T0319027

Cambridge Elements ≡

Elements in Public and Nonprofit Administration
edited by
Andrew Whitford
University of Georgia
Robert Christensen
Brigham Young University

PARTNERSHIP COMMUNITIES

Public–Private Partnerships and Non-Market Infrastructure Development Around the World

Anthony Michael Bertelli
Pennsylvania State University and Institut Barcelona d'Estudis Internacionals

Eleanor Florence Woodhouse
University College London

Michele Castiglioni
European University Institute

Paolo Belardinelli
London School of Economics and Political Science

CAMBRIDGE
UNIVERSITY PRESS

CAMBRIDGE
UNIVERSITY PRESS

University Printing House, Cambridge CB2 8BS, United Kingdom

One Liberty Plaza, 20th Floor, New York, NY 10006, USA

477 Williamstown Road, Port Melbourne, VIC 3207, Australia

314–321, 3rd Floor, Plot 3, Splendor Forum, Jasola District Centre,
New Delhi – 110025, India

103 Penang Road, #05–06/07, Visioncrest Commercial, Singapore 238467

Cambridge University Press is part of the University of Cambridge.

It furthers the University's mission by disseminating knowledge in the pursuit of
education, learning, and research at the highest international levels of excellence.

www.cambridge.org
Information on this title: www.cambridge.org/9781108987431
DOI: 10.1017/9781108987561

First published 2021

A catalogue record for this publication is available from the British Library.

ISBN 978-1-108-98743-1 Paperback
ISSN 2515-4303 (online)
ISSN 2515-429X (print)

Additional resources for this publication at www.cambridge.org/
partnershipcommunities

Partnership Communities

Public–Private Partnerships and Non-Market Infrastructure Development Around the World

Elements in Public and Nonprofit Administration

DOI: 10.1017/9781108987561
First published online: October 2021

Anthony Michael Bertelli
Pennsylvania State University and Institut Barcelona d'Estudis Internacionals

Eleanor Florence Woodhouse
University College London

Michele Castiglioni
European University Institute

Paolo Belardinelli
London School of Economics and Political Science

Author for correspondence: Anthony Michael Bertelli, bertelli@psu.edu

Abstract: We undertake the first quantitative and broadly comparative study of the structure and performance of public-private partnership communities: networked firms that partner with governments to build infrastructure. Our study addresses several important research questions. How connected are the members of partnership communities? How can we understand the quality of the projects a community undertakes? How do political institutions shape their structure and performance? After defining partnership communities as networked communities of private firms that form the consortia that enter into long-term contractual arrangements with governments, we show how they are affected by government demand for partners. We then provide an overview of those factors that predict success in financing projects. Finally, we focus on the political economy of partnership communities. We develop and test theoretical predictions about how national institutions shape partnership communities and the quality of projects. We also investigate voters' preferences over alternative arrangements of infrastructure delivery before drawing out implications for research and practice.

Keywords: infrastructure development, infrastructure finance, political economy, public administration, public–private partnerships

ISBNs: 9781108987431 (PB), 9781108987561 (OC)
ISSNs: 2515-4303 (online), 2515-429X (print)

Contents

A further Online Appendix can be accessed at www.cambridge.org/
partnershipcommunities

1 Partnerships for Infrastructure

In this study, we address the broad question of how private firms and government become intertwined when providing public goods and services. To understand the significance of this question, and the confusing ways in which public and private actors are linked in practice, consider the unenviable task governments have faced in addressing a coronavirus pandemic that had killed more people by the end of 2020 than live in Philadelphia, Pennsylvania. In the United States, the federal response was coordinated through an initiative called Operation Warp Speed, officially described as follows:

> Operation Warp Speed's goal is to produce and deliver 300 million doses of safe and effective vaccines with the initial doses available by January 2021, as part of a broader strategy to accelerate the development, manufacturing, and distribution of COVID-19 vaccines, therapeutics, and diagnostics . . . [It is] a partnership among components of the Department of Health and Human Services . . . including the Centers for Disease Control and Prevention . . . the National Institutes of Health . . . and the Biomedical Advanced Research and Development Authority . . . and the Department of Defense . . . . [Operation Warp Speed] engages with private firms and other federal agencies, including the Department of Veterans Affairs. (US Department of Health and Human Services 2020)

The initiative clearly states that government agencies and private firms constitute a collective effort in order to create and distribute a vaccine. Indeed, a multinational group of pharmaceutical companies including the American Moderna and British AstraZeneca received federal funds to help them to develop and to manufacture a coronavirus vaccine (*New York Times* 2020).

On Monday, November 9, 2020, the pharmaceutical firms Pfizer and BioNTech announced that data from a late-stage clinical trial revealed that their coronavirus vaccine was more than 90% effective (Pfizer Inc. 2020). Four months earlier, Operation Warp Speed had given Pfizer a US$1.95 billion advance-purchase agreement, which was essentially a promise to purchase over 100 million doses of the vaccine when it became ready for safe distribution, but the company received no funding for manufacturing and development (*New York Times* 2020). Pfizer's head of vaccine research and development articulated her understanding of this agreement in an interview that Monday: "We were never part of the Warp Speed . . . we have never taken any money from the U.S. government, or from anyone" (*New York Times* 2020). Vice President Mike Pence thought otherwise, announcing that same morning on Twitter: "HUGE NEWS: Thanks to the public–private partnership forged by President @realDonaldTrump, @pfizer announced its Coronavirus Vaccine trial is EFFECTIVE, preventing infection in 90% of its volunteers." And in the Rose Garden two days later, President Trump claimed credit for the vaccine: "As a result of Operation Warp Speed, Pfizer announced on Monday that its China virus [sic] vaccine is more than 90 percent effective" (White House 2020). What is more, the president's remarks were critical of Pfizer for claiming distance from his administration's signature effort. "Pfizer said it wasn't part of Warp Speed," the president continued, "but that turned out to be an unfortunate misrepresentation. They are part. That's why we gave them the $1.95 million – billion dollars" (White House 2020).

1.1 What Is a Public–Private Partnership?

What are public–private partnerships (PPPs)? Why are they so complex that business and political executives seem to find it difficult to understand and to describe them? For the World Bank, PPPs are defined as long-term contractual arrangements that combine the financing and operation of assets or services that benefit the public. A crucial feature of PPPs is that the private partner "bears significant risk and management responsibility" in the provision of the public asset and "remuneration is linked to performance" (World Bank 2017, 5). In the large literature on PPPs in the scholarly field of public administration, definitions converge on three requirements: (1) some form of cooperation between public- and private-sector organizations; (2) some form of risk sharing between the governments and private-sector organizations involved in an arrangement; and (3) the joint production of public services or assets having public benefit (e.g., Klijn and Teisman 2003; Savas 2000). In the literature, definitional disagreements are not policy neutral. Hodge and Greve (2007, 546) write that scholars seem to divide between those who "view PPPs as a tool of governance and those who think it is a 'language game'" and cast PPPs negatively and in a way reminiscent of the debates about privatization or contracting.

Two crucial elements of understanding PPPs are time and risk allocation. Forrer et al. (2010, 476) contend that for an arrangement to be considered a PPP, it must be that (1) "[t]he relationship between the public and the private sector organization is long term, rather than a one-time relationship" and that (2) the arrangement "involves a negotiated allocation of risk between the public and private sectors, instead of government bearing most of the risk." Those close to the practice agree. The PPP advisor to the Ministry of Finance of Uzbekistan told Cece (2020, 27) that "short term contracts are not PPP . . . the time horizon is important." The head of the Sustainable Infrastructure Policy Unit at the European Bank for Reconstruction and Development believed that a requirement is that "the private party bears significant risk and management responsibility throughout the life of the contract" (27). Moreover, the senior

PPP specialist at the World Bank similarly related the additional requirement that "more risk is taken by the private partner than the public partner in a PPP" (27).

Longevity and privately borne risk lie at the heart of this study. Interestingly, because of its focus on a single virus, Operation Warp Speed seems unlikely to meet the longevity criterion of our working definition of a PPP, even though risk allocation does take place in the agreements between the US government and pharmaceutical manufacturers.

1.2 Building Infrastructure through Partnerships

In the pages that follow, our focus will be on partnerships that create assets, specifically infrastructure, rather than public services. We call them *partnerships for infrastructure*. For some, what constitutes infrastructure may be as difficult to define as PPPs. At the end of March 2021, President Biden announced a $2 trillion plan to restore and enhance infrastructure in the United States. The plan was quickly attacked by Republicans for considering spending on affordable housing, care for the elderly and disabled, and the replacement of lead pipes for water supply as being outside of the definition of infrastructure. "When people think about infrastructure," said Senator Roy Blunt (R-MO) "they're thinking about roads, bridges, ports and airports" (Tankersley and Smialek 2021). Said a befuddled South Dakota Governor Kristi Noem: "I was shocked by how much doesn't go into infrastructure," noting that the money in President Biden's plan "goes into research and development, it goes into housing and pipes and different initiatives, green energy" (Sheffey 2021). White House senior advisor Anita Dunn shot back: "We think that the people in Jackson, [Mississippi], might be surprised to hear that fixing that water system doesn't count as infrastructure. We think the people of Texas might disagree with the idea that the electric grid isn't infrastructure that needs to be built with resilience for the 21st century" (Tankersley and Smialek 2021). While our sample does not include social programs such as elder care, it is more expansive than the Blunt–Noem consensus. Partnerships for infrastructure build, restore, and operate the highways, bridges, waste management sites, and the energy plants that improve citizens' quality of life and stimulate economic development.

As shown in Figure 1, our data reveal significant variation between 1990 and 2020 in the types of assets that are delivered through partnerships across the regions of the world. Wind, solar, and roads are popular sectors in Europe, followed by schools and combined-cycle gas turbine (CCGT) power plants. In the Americas, the picture is similar except that gas projects are also frequently

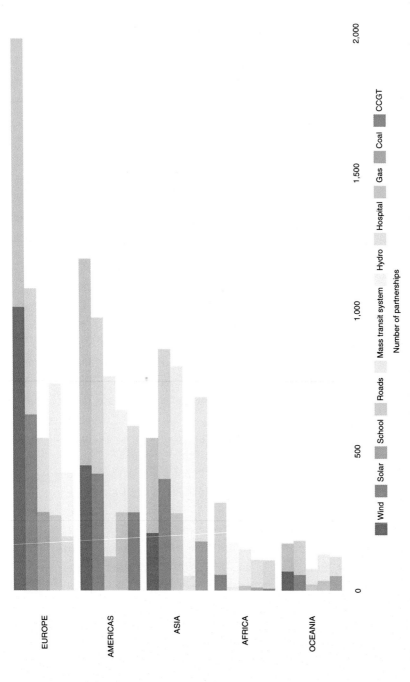

Figure 1 Partnerships for infrastructure by sector and region, 1990–2020. Source: SDC Platinum database. Top-five sectors only. Number of financed projects in full shade, number of announced projects in faded shade.

delivered using partnerships for infrastructure. In the other regions of the world, the distributions are more idiosyncratic, reflecting the various needs of these regions. Solar, roads, and coal are the most popular sectors in Asia, with wind coming in closely behind. In Africa and Oceania, energy projects such as wind and solar also lead the way. And one cannot ignore the difference in magnitude across regions, with the top five of the 193 nations in our study – the United States, United Kingdom, Australia, India, and Brazil – accounting for 33% of all announced projects.

1.3 The Microeconomics behind Partnerships

The advantage of using partnerships rather than public administration to build infrastructure for microeconomic theorists lies in "bundling" construction and management such that a single consortium of private partners bears the risks for both phases (Engel, Fischer, and Galetovic 2014). By giving the consortium responsibility for building and operating, it has strong incentives to build well because it will be responsible for operating the asset for a significant amount of time. In this way, the very long duration of PPP contracts discussed earlier strengthens the incentives of the consortium to build or rehabilitate an asset in a sound way: a portion of their returns on the asset will depend upon its performance over decades.

An extensive literature analyzing the costs and benefits of partnerships for infrastructure constructs a more sanguine view of the strength of these incentives. They can only be enjoyed under certain conditions. For example, a better made bridge is less likely to need repairs ten years down the line. Bundling here is sensible as it mitigates moral hazard: if the same consortium will be maintaining the bridge well after its construction, it has a clear incentive to build it well (Martimort and Pouyet 2008). Now consider that building a more efficient water purification system is one thing, but operating it involves learning a vast amount about management, and that learning imposes a cost of operation. In this scenario, the agency problems at each stage – building and operating – do not improve inefficiency – that is, mitigating moral hazard in building makes the same problem in operating worse. Bundling does not improve efficiency and each phase of the water purification project should have its own consortium (Martimort and Pouyet 2008).

When compared against the benchmark of construction and management by the public sector, many things influence whether or not a PPP makes sense for building infrastructure. Recent work by the microeconomic theorists Elisabetta Iossa and David Martimort has revealed many important theoretical factors. Agency costs accrue for the government when project management is effectively delegated to a private consortium (Iossa and Martimort 2012) – that is, the theoretical problem is similar to the problem of delegating to public agencies (e.g., Huber and Shipan 2002). Whether demand for the benefits of the asset is stable and easy to forecast also impacts the efficiency of bundling (Iossa and Martimort 2015). Moreover, if the government can write a more-or-less complete contract with the consortium, the influence of corruption within existing public administration can be lessened (Iossa and Martimort 2016; but see Bertelli, Mele, and Woodhouse 2020).

In many countries and political jurisdictions, partnerships for infrastructure are often the only feasible option for delivering large-scale infrastructure projects given the ability that these governments have to raise money (Yehoue, Hammami, and Ruhashyankiko 2006). Like bond issues, partnerships for infrastructure allow governments to build infrastructure on credit. But because important risks associated with the project are fully borne by the private consortium, its investments do not count against government budget deficits (Ball, Heafey, and King 2001). Indeed, governments have had a penchant for front-loading investment obligations onto private consortia, leaving the government itself with essentially no up-front costs (Post 2014). Regardless of whether or not a PPP offers efficiency gains, it may be more attractive to some governments because it shows them a way to deliver infrastructure without affecting their current balance sheets.

1.4 The Popularity of Partnerships for Infrastructure

The promise of efficiently delivering infrastructure with substantial help from the private sector and without engaging in normal budgetary politics has made partnerships for infrastructure incredibly popular across the globe, and among national and subnational levels of government. European countries increased fivefold their use of PPPs from 1990 to the mid-2000s, when the growth trajectory slowed through 2011 (Engel, Fischer, and Galetovic 2014, 4). Low- and middle-income countries, by contrast, saw investment in partnerships for infrastructure grow by a yearly average of 28.3% from 1990 to 1997. After a slow period during the Asian financial crisis, "a new growth spurt" began in 2003 and continued through the end of the first decade of the twenty-first century (4). In 2019, global investment levels in partnerships for infrastructure showed a 14% increase compared to 2018 and an 18% increase over the averages of the previous five years (World Bank 2019). What is more, in 2014, 59% of investment in partnerships for infrastructure occurring in OECD countries was made at the subnational level (OECD 2018). According to more recent data, this trend seems to have remained stable (if not slightly increased). In 2019, locally sponsored projects accounted for almost two-thirds (63%) of the total number of projects recorded in the first half of 2019 (World Bank 2019).

Two pre-construction stages of PPPs will play an important role in this study. The announcement of a project indicates that the government is looking for a consortium of private partners. The financing of a project is a condition met when the private partners have raised the funds needed to develop the asset in question and the government matching funds, if any, are in place. Consortia of partners typically invest in a special-purpose vehicle (SPV), which has the single purpose of signing the long-term contract with the government for the project that was announced. The SPV handles all cash flows from the investments of consortium of partners, loans, and, eventually, the income from the use of the asset in the operating phase (Moore, Boardman, and Vining 2017, 210; Ng and Loosemore 2007, 9).[1]

Categorized by region of the world, Figure 2 shows the annual numbers of announced and financed projects in the data that we use in this study both globally and by region. As is to be expected, the number of financed partnerships for infrastructure is significantly lower than the number announced. But what is clear is that these partnerships have been growing in popularity consistently since the 1990s. The dashed gray line represents the number of global announced projects and the solid gray line represents financed projects worldwide. In Europe and Asia, partnerships for infrastructure have been highly successful in attracting investors since the early 2000s. The Americas, instead, became more successful in attracting investors in the mid-2010s (all regions experienced a drop in project financing in 2008 when the global financial crisis struck). The attraction of capital to partnerships for infrastructure is a crucial issue in understanding their promise for economic development worldwide.[2]

1.5 A New Focus: Partnership Communities

To date, the overwhelming focus of the literature on partnerships for infrastructure has been on individual projects, with qualitative accounts digging deep into their details and quantitative studies taking them as the unit of analysis for large-scale examination. We depart from this approach in an important way. At the heart of this study is the question of how the private firms involved in

---

[1] This practice is in evidence in the data we employ in this study. In approximately 95% of projects, the company managing the project is an SPV, not a financial sponsor. The very small number of remaining projects have large corporations in a management and financing role.

[2] In Figure 2, the graph kinks downward for the last available years in the data set. This is due to several factors, the main one being the timing of data collection, as the last projects entering our database (May 21, 2020) have not had time to be financed.

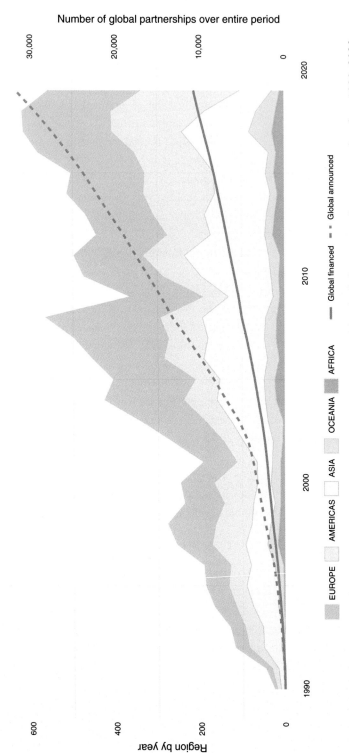

Figure 2 Number of announced and financed (global and regional) partnerships for infrastructure by sector and region, 1990–2020.

Source: SDC Platinum database.

partnerships are interconnected, globally and domestically. We focus on partnership communities, and we examine how the marketplace for partners is structured within countries and across the world. This reframing helps us to overcome a major theoretical hurdle for understanding the supply of private partners, rather than simply their demand by governments.

Partnership communities are networked groups of private firms that form the consortia that enter into long-term contractual arrangements with governments. One of the main concerns about the market for partners is limited competition among private companies for bidding on announced projects, even in those markets, like the United Kingdom, where the number of successfully financed partnerships is relatively very high (Carrillo et al. 2008). The costs of bidding on announced projects, favoritism, and even a lack of efficiency gains from competitive bidding create a reality in which governments lack real choice among partners (cf. Bajari, Houghton, and Tadelis 2014; Bajari, McMillan, and Tadelis 2009; Coviello and Mariniello 2014; de Silva et al. 2008; Guasch 2004; Ohashi 2009). As markets for partners become less competitive, the private interests of the partners can become powerful enough to take precedence over the public interest (Herics et al. 2018). This is the non-market aspect of infrastructure development worldwide. It is essential to understand the interconnections between partners that both create and restrict the opportunities for governments.

How private interests organize around the delivery of public goods is crucial to understand our present context. Infrastructure is one of the fundamental ingredients for competitive industries to thrive, and its provision and upkeep is of the utmost importance for the competitiveness and economic success of nations (Porter 1990). Consequently, we take inspiration from Porter's (1998) theory of clusters, groupings of interconnected firms that are proximate in geography, in developing the partnership community as a group of potential and real partners for the government when it announces its desire to create a partnership for infrastructure. In Section 2, we estimate the number and characteristics of partnership communities across nations and time using concepts and methods from network analysis.

1.6 An Overview of the Study

To understand our argument, imagine a first phase in which a pathbreaking firm works with a government to create a demand for partners in infrastructure development. As Porter (1990; 1998) recognized, this firm can use local talent advantages to exploit economies of scale and scope in a second phase, attracting investment along the way. A third phase then reveals the partnership community, in which the pathbreaking firm can marshal investors into a consortium and manage the partnership through its own contracts with more specialized firms with talent advantages. In this way, the partnership community of the pathbreaking, specialized, and additional firms providing private investment in PPPs becomes essential for the government to extract the efficiency and political benefits of these projects. Far from developing a more competitive marketplace, we expect the number of partnership communities to *diminish* as more partnerships for infrastructure are announced within a country. We find support for this claim in Section 2.

Our focus then turns to projects. What makes some projects "better" than others? As important as it is, the question of performance in long-term arrangements like partnerships for infrastructure is a tricky one. While the literature is replete with accounts of problematic projects (e.g., Chen, Hubbard, and Liao 2013) and discussions of the criteria for successful partnerships are many (e.g., Vining and Boardman 2008; Zhang 2005), the ultimate criterion of PPP failure – their cancellation – is a very rare event (Bertelli, Mele, and Whitford 2020). We view success through a political lens, and focus on the pre-construction phase, when political credit for launching infrastructure development is possible if a deal can be struck (Bertelli 2019). Our performance metric draws on a view of "good" partners as accelerating projects, rather than completing them (Guzman and Stern 2015). It ascribes greater quality to *present* projects when their partners have successfully moved *past* projects from announcement to financing. Financing is the crucial step in privately financed infrastructure; it is the moment when the promise of private capital can finally be leveraged for providing public goods. For politicians, it is a crucial moment too because incumbents can claim credit for the promise of what a partnership for infrastructure is expected to deliver (Bertelli 2019). Consequently, we examine the quality of projects from their launch, not, say, at the end of lengthy construction and operation phases. Our strategy for creating this metric is detailed in Section 3.

Partnerships for infrastructure are politically important, and because the rich literatures of political economy show that institutions shape both politics and economic activity, institutions surely matter in our context. Armed with measures of communities and the quality of the projects to which they contribute, we explore an argument that democracy and the rule of law are responsible for the development of partnership communities and the distribution of quality projects. We show that a minimal concept of democracy – that it is participatory and that power is contestable – is not enough to understand how democratic politics influences partnerships for infrastructure. Our focusing on relevant aspects of political and judicial institutions produces evidence consistent with a series of claims about the predictability of the environment for partnership development. The risk to projects from the potential for partisan change in government is associated with lower quality but stronger communities to mitigate that risk. Corruption in the courts and the bureaucracy influence project quality and communities in very different ways. While broad perceptions that the rule of law adheres in a country are associated with higher-quality projects, judicial corruption invites weaker partnership communities. Side payments to the bureaucracy may well make bureaucratic application of rules to projects more predictable, but communities in countries where this is common form tighter linkages among partners to hedge risk. What is more, where pork-barrel politics is common, project quality is lower and partnership communities are stronger, but when government has a residual claim to an asset that enhances the potential for credit claiming (Bertelli 2019), quality is higher. Overall, the structure of national politics cannot be ignored, and its influence helps the network of partners to congeal into something quite distinct from a competitive marketplace.

Partnerships for infrastructure likely would be less appealing to politicians if citizens did not use the means of public goods provision when deciding which candidate deserves their votes. That is, it is crucial to understand whether the PPP as a form of public goods provision actually impacts the choices of voters. We ask whether partnerships for infrastructure influence citizens' thinking about electoral accountability to explore a mechanism that underlies important aspects of the institutional politics just described. Section 5 presents evidence that PPPs might be a very effective way for politicians to enhance vote share from providing public goods. Evidence from a survey experiment in the United States shows that partnerships are associated with a greater likelihood of voting for an incumbent member of Congress, but only before the project is completed. Once the infrastructure is in place, voters are influenced by the performance of the asset in delivering public benefits, not the actors – private or public – involved.

Our study shows that developing strong partnership communities is attractive to politicians who face the reality of being sanctioned by voters, and relying on them can positively influence voters' perceptions about how well an asset ultimately will do in delivering the benefits politicians promise when announcing its construction. This observation has a variety of policy and management implications as well as pathways for future research, which we explore in Section 6. In short, epistemic communities inspired by New Public Management (NPM) that advocate the potential of partnership communities are not misguided, but they cannot ignore the influence of national political and legal institutions on the attractiveness – and the success – of partnerships for infrastructure in political decision-making.

2 Conceptualizing Partnership Communities

Our concept of partnership communities has two crucial features. First, they exist within a network of linked private firms within a country. Second, those links are associated with the long-term contractual arrangements with governments that are essential to how we define partnerships for infrastructure. Network analysis has become a crucial tool for understanding the structures of public management and how they relate to political institutions (e.g., Milward and Provan 1998). For the purpose of our quantitative analysis, we will define a node in these national networks as a firm participating in *any* partnership. The links among these firms, or edges in the language of network analysis, are commercial relations, which exist when firms work together on a single partnership. These building blocks will allow us to visualize national networks, to quantitatively characterize key aspects of them, and to apply a set of criteria to define *partnership communities* within those networks. After presenting our data and discussing the methods by which we do these things, we will test Hypothesis 1 – the number of communities decreases as countries adopt more partnerships for infrastructure – to conclude the section.

2.1 Data

Our data are extracted from the Thompson Reuters Securities Data Company (SDC) Platinum Database, a database of historical financial transactions that has information on partnerships that has been used in prior academic studies (e.g., Quelin et al. 2019). The resulting data set used in this study contains information on 32,319 infrastructure partnerships, of which we are able to use 26,781 due to certain partnerships missing information, involving 20,225 companies that cover all countries across the globe. This is the most extensive and comprehensive data set of partnerships for infrastructure available to the best of our knowledge.

Table 1 illustrates the scope of our data on the projects produced through partnerships for infrastructure, broadly speaking. There is much variation in terms of the yearly coverage of countries. The total number of projects announced and financed illustrates the patterns shown in Figure 2 in the preceding section, particularly the inter-regional inequity in adopting partnerships for infrastructure, particularly when comparing Africa and Oceania with the other regions of the world. The percentage of announced projects that become financed shows striking differences as well, with African partnerships being successfully financed at a rate of less than half of those in Europe, and British partnerships attracting private investment nearly six times more frequently than Chinese comparators. The shortest average time to financing is the eight months it takes for projects in

Table 1 Partnerships for infrastructure descriptive statistics.

	Years	Project announced	Project financed (% within five years of being announced)	Project financed (%)	Time financed (months)	Number of companies	Average cost (million $US)	Number of sectors	Number of subsectors
World	1940–2020	2,6781	36.51	37.99	13.35	20,225	940.64	11	87
Europe	1973–2020	7,435	49.78	51.63	12.71	6,212	571.73	11	81
Americas	1972–2020	7,974	33.26	34.04	10.94	6,134	844.51	11	85
Asia	1973–2020	8,041	31.26	33.12	15.57	6,813	1,258.04	11	78
Oceania	1940–2020	1,611	35.75	37.18	15.64	1,517	1,159.31	11	75
Africa	1972–2020	1,720	19.48	20.93	18.06	1,978	1,351.84	11	72
United States	1972–2020	3,345	40.57	41.2	7.89	2,528	912.52	11	75

Table 1 (cont.)

	Years	Project announced	Project financed (% within five years of being announced)	Project financed (%)	Time financed (months)	Number of companies	Average cost (million $US)	Number of sectors	Number of subsectors
China	1973–2020	1,192	9.23	9.82	18.97	1,165	1,558.6	11	62
Australia	1940–2020	1,485	36.09	37.51	15.79	1,375	1,188.08	11	73
India	1981–2020	1,508	44.03	45.76	11.02	1,109	953.76	11	61
Brazil	1990–2020	1,211	23.62	24.28	10.96	1,000	1,025.61	10	60
United Kingdom	1984–2020	1,840	54.4	57.28	19.38	1,638	582.46	11	63
Russia	1990–2020	360	25.56	26.67	14.92	458	2,156.13	10	50
Canada	1988–2020	739	35.86	36.81	13.04	781	1,001.7	10	61

| Indonesia | 1978–2020 | 712 | 19.94 | 21.91 | 26.53 | 755 | 1,054.41 | 10 | 55 |
| Saudi Arabia | 1995–2020 | 209 | 33.01 | 33.01 | 17.25 | 247 | 3,443.86 | 9 | 39 |

These ten individual countries have the highest absolute value partnerships in the database used for this study. All other countries are reported on in the online appendix, Table A1. **Source:** Thompson Reuters Securities Data Company.

the United States, which is less than half the speed of British partnerships. The United States also leads the world in the number of firms involved in partnerships for infrastructure, with double the firms involved in China, and nearly ten times those in Saudi Arabia. By contrast, and on average, the highest project valuations are in Saudi Arabia, where they are almost six times the average value of British projects. Finally, the United States also leads the world in terms of the biggest range of sectors and subsectors for which partnerships for infrastructure are used (eleven sectors and seventy-five subsectors), compared with Saudi Arabia where nine sectors and thirty-nine subsectors are covered. We note additionally that the modal type of PPP employed is a Build-Own-Operate (BOO) agreement, under which ownership remains with the consortium of partners at the end of the long-term contract.

2.2 Networks of Partners

These data catalog individual projects from which we extract information about the partners involved in them. Partner-level data are used to estimate the networks of partners that lie at the core of our analytic strategy. As with many other applications of network analysis in public management research (e.g., Binz-Scharf et al. 2012), we can see which private partners are involved in which projects, and we can model patterns of collaboration among them.

Each network of partners is composed of *nodes*, which represent the firms that contribute to a project. For instance, a project for building bridge X may involve three private partners, A, B, and C, which appear as separate nodes in the network of partners. Nodes are connected to one another via *edges*, which represent *commercial relationships* between firms with regard to specific projects. These are likely to be a mix of formal and relational contracts (e.g., Bertelli and Smith 2010), but our data limits us to identifying firms that participate in the same project, so we use a more general term when describing them. Continuing our example, A, B, and C are all connected by edges, but they would not be connected to firm D, which worked on a separate project to build toll road Y. D appears as an unlinked node, or a disconnected *component*, in the network because there is no path linking D to the component on project X (including nodes A, B, and C) along any edge.

Figure 3 graphically represents a "toy" example of a network of partners. The dots (nodes) represent private partners that are connected by lines (edges) to other partners in a partnership for infrastructure project. When a firm has a commercial relationship with multiple firms on different projects, components become connected to one another, as Figure 3 shows. In the southeast of that panel are two additional components, having four and two nodes respectively.

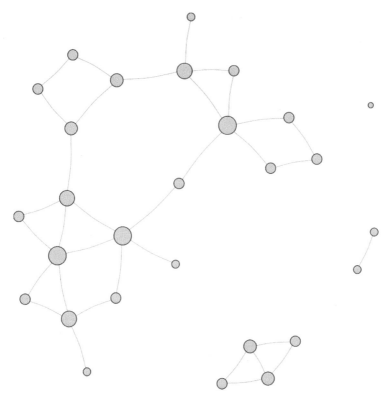

Figure 3 Example of a network. Dots represent nodes, lines represent edges.

These may represent partners with no commercial relationships with sponsors in the main component of the network. In the northeast is a single disconnected component, or singleton, as with firm D in our example.

The *size* of a network is the number of nodes with which it is composed. In our data, Somalia has no real network at all because it has only one partner in the database.[3] In Table 2 (columns 2–10), the basic characteristics of regional networks of partners, as well as those for the top-ten countries in PPP value (as in Table 1) are presented. The United States leads the world with 2,528 nodes, followed by the United Kingdom with 1,638. The number of edges in the networks of partners in our sample ranges from one – for example, the singleton in Somalia – to 2,939 in the United States.

The *number of components* is the number of subgroups of nodes all connected along a path of edges within a network, or the number of independent parts of which a network is composed. Given that the number of components is

---

[3] Country level statistics are presented in the online appendix, Table A2.

Table 2 Characteristics of networks of partners.

	Nodes	Edges	Components	Largest component (%)	Ratio of components: nodes	Diameter	Density	Clustering coefficient	Centrali -zation	Number of communities	Average number of members	Modularity
World	20,226	34,482	7,312	0.53	0.36	15	0.00017	0.19	0.04	555	17.94	0.84
Europe	6,212	10,181	2,151	0.52	0.35	13	0.00053	0.28	0.03	224	14.23	0.84
Americas	6,135	8,428	2,445	0.46	0.40	13	0.00045	0.36	0.03	225	12.13	0.87
Asia	6,813	11,023	2,475	0.49	0.36	23	0.00048	0.26	0.05	258	13.47	0.86
Africa	1,978	2,758	750	0.43	0.38	17	0.00141	0.46	0.04	104	9.8	0.85
Oceania	1,517	2,329	534	0.5	0.35	13	0.00203	0.35	0.04	67	11.52	0.81
United States	2,528	2,939	1,065	0.4	0.42	14	0.00092	0.52	0.03	114	9.04	0.90
China	1,165	972	612	0.2	0.53	12	0.00143	0.53	0.02	72	5.67	0.90
Australia	1,375	2,035	496	0.49	0.36	13	0.00215	0.34	0.04	64	10.73	0.81
India	1,109	1,061	511	0.25	0.46	14	0.00173	0.48	0.02	74	6.16	0.84
Brazil	1,000	1,303	409	0.4	0.41	12	0.00261	0.41	0.03	60	7.55	0.60

United Kingdom	1,638	2,841	481	0.59	0.29	14	0.00212	0.32	0.08	71	13.51	0.83
Russia	458	665	187	0.34	0.41	14	0.00635	0.54	0.04	29	7.86	0.62
Canda	781	1,431	282	0.48	0.36	15	0.0047	0.53	0.08	34	11.74	0.72
Indonesia	755	1,152	210	0.52	0.28	11	0.00405	0.31	0.16	49	9.39	0.79
Saudi Arabia	247	417	66	0.53	0.27	9	0.01373	0.52	0.10	18	8.61	0.75

The ten individual countries have the highest average value partnerships in the database used for this study. All other countries are reported on in the online appendix, Table A2. **Source:** Thompson Reuters Securities Data Company.

generally a function of both network size and the clustering of nodes, an across-country comparison can be made by looking at the *ratio of components to nodes*: this varies significantly among our top-ten countries in Table 2, where China leads with a ratio of 0.53, and Saudi Arabia lags with 0.27.

The *distance* between two nodes is the number of edges between two nodes. A *path* connects two nodes without traveling through any node or along any edge more than once. Thus, if A works on a project with B, and B works on a project with C, but A and C do not work on a project together, the path length between A and C is 2. The *diameter* of a network measures how compact, or efficient, it is by identifying the "longest of the shortest paths" across all pairs of nodes (Newman 2018, 132, 399). For disconnected networks, the longest diameter is generally that of the largest component. In the top-ten countries that were reported in Table 2, the *share* of total sponsors that belong to the *largest component* in the network ranges from 20% (China) to 59% (United Kingdom). In countries with singleton nodes, the diameter is 0, while it is highest in Canada (15) and lowest in Saudi Arabia (9) among our top-ten countries.

The *density* of a network refers to the proportion of observed ties between nodes among all possible ties. These numbers are small because the number of possible ties is quite large – in a simple network of 100 nodes, the maximum number of ties is 4,950. The density of our national networks, which can be considered the chance that two randomly selected nodes are connected with an edge (Newman 2018, 128), is significantly larger in Saudi Arabia than in the rest of the top-ten countries.

The *clustering coefficient* measures the probability that the nodes adjacent to a given node are connected. This is equivalent to the existence of a transitive relation between nodes; that is to say, to paraphrase the saying about friends, the partner of my partner is also my partner (Newman 2018, 183). It is thus appropriate that the worldwide network of partners has a much lower clustering coefficient (0.19) than the networks in China, Russia, or Saudi Arabia (all greater than 0.5). Consider a "triangle" that connects Russian firms A and B with one edge and B and C with one edge. A and C are more than twice as likely to also be connected in the Russian network than they are in the larger European network. This provides some suggestion that the Russian network might be considered "denser" than that of Europe.

A final property we consider is *centralization*, or "the tendency of a single point to be more central than all other points in the network" (Freeman et al. 1979, 227). Whereas centrality (we use betweenness centrality) is a measure of nodes, centralization is a measure of inequality under this dimension (Hanneman and Riddle 2005). Measures of centralization are "based on differences between the centrality of the most central point and that of all others" (227). In Rwanda, Guyana, and Tunisia, our centralization measure is 0, meaning that firms only work on projects alone – and would be 1 if there were a network structured in the shape of a star. The Indonesian and Saudi Arabian networks are the most centralized among the top-ten countries as determined by the value of their partnerships for infrastructure.

2.3 Partnership Communities

We rely on the tools of network analysis to detect partnership communities. This section presents a general overview of the process of community detection in our study, while a detailed description appears in Section 3 of the online appendix.

Communities are constituent parts of a larger network that is more densely connected internally than with the rest of the network. It is important to detect communities and to treat them as distinct entities because they can have properties that differ substantially from those of the network as a whole. As the physicist Mark Newman (2006, 1) puts it, studies "that focus on whole networks and ignore community structure may miss many interesting features."

How do communities stand out from a larger network? The answer can be seen in Figure 4, which depicts the identical network that appears in Figure 3 (left panel). But this time, distinct communities are highlighted in the yellow, orange, purple, and pink areas (right panel). The hallmarks of a network with communities are quickly apparent: they have denser internal connections among the firms within, but sparser connections between, communities. Our claim is that the networks of partners in countries of the world are organized into communities like these, and that this feature suggests that the relationship among partners is not one of market competition.

When detecting communities,[4] we simplify the overall network of partners in a theoretically meaningful way. Our first step is to consider for inclusion in communities only those sponsors with at least two commercial relations.[5] The reasons for this are twofold. First, we want to exclude firms with no project ties

---

[4] Community structure is detected using a multi-level modularity optimization algorithm (Blondel et al. 2008). The algorithm, known as the "Louvain method," is considered state-of-the-art for large network community detection. We account for partnerships developed over the whole coverage period, considering time and project cost as weights – where more recent and more costly projects are given more weight. Details and robustness tests are provided in the online appendix, Section 3.

[5] This amounts to a k-core decomposition, with $k = 2$. The "pruning" produces subgraphs where each vertex is connected to at least two other vertices. The community detection algorithm is performed on the subgraphs.

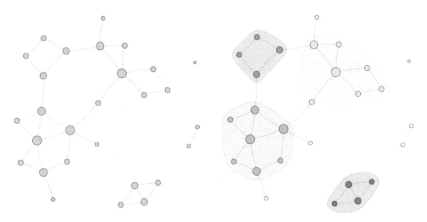

Figure 4 Example of a network with communities. Dots represent nodes, lines represent edges, shaded areas in color represent communities.

to any other firm, or those that work with another firm only once. The exclusions are illustrated by the single dot and the two dots connected by a single edge on the southeast side of Figure 4. While these two exclusions adhere to a definition appropriate for network analysis – they are constituent parts of a larger network that are more densely connected internally – neither fits our substantive definition of a partnership community. We have defined partnership communities as networked communities of private firms that form the consortia that enter into long-term contractual arrangements with governments. A singleton firm shares risk with the government, which can be defined as a *contractual* relationship. A community of firms shares risk both with the government and, crucially among other firms. When only one edge connects two nodes, the situation represents a bilateral contract between two firms that collectively share risk with the government. This comes closer to the idea of a community. Yet, crucially, all risk is allocated in a single contract, and the relationship is better conceived as such. Adding a third firm would allow the risk sharing to involve different relationships among the partners; risk can be shared in a complex arrangement that involves the government. The communities highlighted in the right panel of Figure 4 fit our definition. Long-term arrangements between government and these communities are distinctive to the extent to which risk can be shared among the partners and the relative distinctiveness among these communities as potential collective agents with which government can enter into partnerships for infrastructure.

Table 2 (columns 11–13) reports network statistics for partnership communities, reported according to geographical area. *Communities* counts the total number of communities detected in a given country, which varies from a low of 18 in Saudi Arabia to a high of 114 in the United States among our top-ten countries. The United Kingdom has the largest communities (13.51) of our top-ten countries, whereas China and India have the smallest average communities (5.67 and 6.16, respectively). *Modularity*, instead, is a measure of the extent to which like is connected to like in a network (Newman 2018, 205), where positive values (strictly less than 1) indicate assortative mixing, or put differently, mixing based on similar characteristics. Thus, it captures the extent to which there is mixing within communities in a country. For example, in our top-ten countries, China and the United States display the highest (0.90) assortative matching between communities, and Brazil the lowest (0.59). This implies that Chinese and American communities tend to be more inward-looking in that they collaborate more with members from the same community, whereas Brazilian communities display more cross-fertilization across communities.

2.4 Partnership Communities Up Close

Three things are important to observe about partnership communities in order to grasp them intuitively. First, it is crucial to understand how real networks are represented by the graphics we have been considering. Second, empirically speaking, partnership communities consolidate over time. Third, various types of firms comprise partnership communities. In this section, we look at the partnership community of the Royal Bank of Scotland (RBS), one of the most active financial sponsors in the United Kingdom. Figure 5 shows the bank's partnership communities over time, from 1995 to 2015 in ten-year increments. We distinguish between financial firms (square nodes) and other types of firms (circle nodes).

The first snapshot shows RBS in 1995 as part of a small partnership community (diameter: 4, size: 21) and playing a relatively marginal role (within-community degree: 8, normalized betweenness: 0.096). In the second, the community has enlarged over the intervening ten years (diameter: 9, order: 143) and RBS plays a more central role (within-community degree: 34, normalized betweenness: 0.293). In the third, the community in 2015 has become the largest in the United Kingdom (diameter: 9, order: 292 – comprising 34.6% of sponsors in the market) and RBS plays an even more central role (within-community degree: 47, normalized betweenness: 0.312). The involvement of RBS in its partnership community – calculated as the share of within-community collaborations over total collaborations, inside and outside the community – grows over time from 61.5% to 70.1%. In other words, RBS becomes increasingly involved with firms that are already part of its community

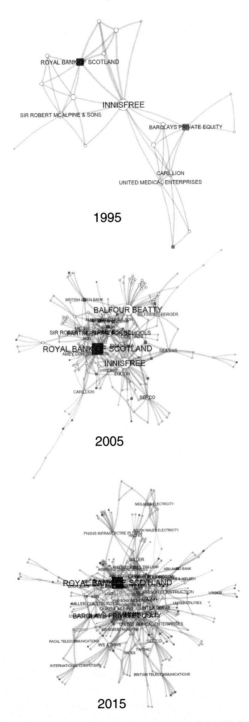

Figure 5 The partnership community of RBS of the United Kingdom (1995, 2005, and 2015). Square nodes represent financial firms and circle

Caption for Figure 5 (cont.)

> nodes represent other types of firms. The size of the node represents the
> degree of the node (how many partners it has). The thickness of the edge
> represents the value of the contract.

as time passes. Over the course of two decades, the partnership community grows, it becomes less centralized, and the share of its financial partners (including that of RBS) increases from 14.3% to 17.1%.

In short, the case of RBS shows that as the partnership community consolidates over time, RBS becomes more dominant within the community. This seems to be a trend in the United Kingdom in general, with dominant players acquiring a disproportionately central role in communities over time. This could be because dominant firms become better at bidding for contracts as their experience grows. It might also happen because the government has confidence in firms with which it has worked with in the past. This is something that we hope that future research will address.

2.5 Partnership Communities Compared

We now turn our attention to comparing partnership communities across national contexts. By focusing on two countries that rely extensively on partnerships for infrastructure, the United States and United Kingdom, we can visually examine the differences in the structure of their partnership communities. Figure 6 shows a comparison of the networks in these two nations in 2005. What is immediately clear from looking at each panel is that that the United Kingdom has a network structure (right panel) that is much more interconnected than that of the United States (left panel). This observation is borne out by network and community statistics in 2005. The two countries had networks of a similar size, the United States with 999 and the United Kingdom with 883 nodes, respectively. However, the United Kingdom had significantly more edges (USA: 1,481 vs. UK: 1,871), fewer components (USA: 360 vs. UK: 177), a shorter diameter of the largest component (USA: 20 vs. GBR: 10), as well as higher density (USA: 0.0029 vs. UK: 0.0048) and centralization scores (USA: 0.045 vs. UK: 0.109) than the United States.

These kinds of comparisons between partnership community structures across countries lie at the heart of our theoretical argument about the role of institutions. But before addressing those claims, we must address an additional source of variation – that is, across time.

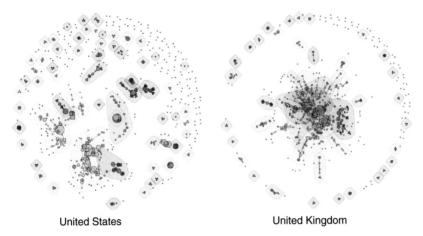

United States   United Kingdom

Figure 6 Partnership communities in the United States (left panel) and
United Kingdom (right panel), 2005. Square nodes represent financial firms
and circle nodes represent other types of firms. The size of the node represents
the degree of the node (how many partners it has). The thickness of the
edge represents the value of the contract. The shaded areas demarcate
partnership communities.

2.6 Project Growth and the Evolution of Partnership Communities

The first claim in our theory of partnership communities relates to their development within countries and over time. Before making any inferences, it is useful to
examine such changes graphically as we have done throughout this section. In
Figure 7, it becomes clear that the centralized structure of the network that we
saw in in Figure 6 had already emerged in the late 1990s. This coincides exactly
with the (in)famous New Labour policy about partnerships (or private finance
initiatives, PFI): "PFI or bust" (House of Commons 1997). Essentially, government policy made private financing the mechanism for the delivery of public
infrastructure. This strategy continued through George Osborne's term as
Chancellor of the Exchequer (2010–2016), and so did the controversy that
arose from a government trend to heavily invest in partnerships for infrastructure
despite mounting evidence that the financing mechanism was not providing
value for money (Sparrow 2011). During the years of New Labour governments,
with their exuberance over partnerships for infrastructure depicted in Figure 7,
the development of communities seems to track the number of projects fairly
well. In 1995, 86 projects were financed by the communities in the top left
quadrant, rising to 280 in 2000 for the top right, 575 in 2005 for the bottom left,
and 751 in the bottom right for 2010. More centralized communities, with more
interconnected firms, came to manage a rapidly increasing number of projects.

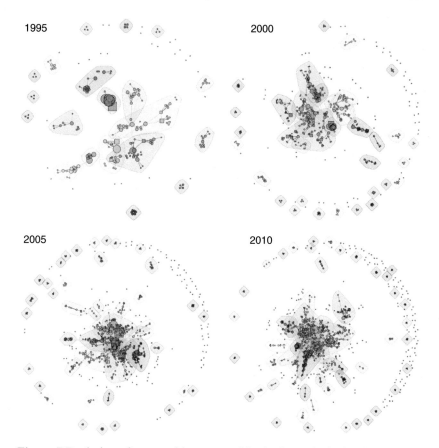

Figure 7 Evolution of partnership communities in the United Kingdom, 1995–2010. Running clockwise from top left, the figure shows the networks of partners for 1995, 2000, 2005, and 2010. Square nodes represent financial firms and circle nodes represent other types of firms. The size of the node represents the degree of the node (how many partners it has). The thickness of the edge represents the value of the contract. The shaded areas demarcate partnership communities.

The pattern in the United Kingdom is all the more striking if we compare it with that in the United States for the same years, as shown in Figure 8. With far more decentralized decision-making due to its federalism, American networks look very different. Moving clockwise from the top left quadrant, the communities depicted financed 89 (1995), 267 (2000), 403 (2005), and 624 (2010) projects, respectively. The number of financed projects in both the United Kingdom and the United States more than quadrupled between 1992 and 1998, and two different network structures were able to generate the consortia

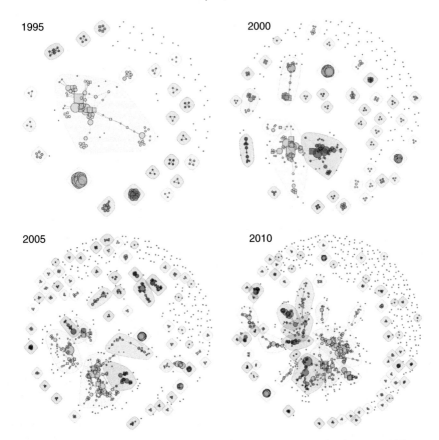

1995

2000

2005

2010

Figure 8 Evolution of partnership communities in the United States, 1995–2010. Running clockwise from top left, the figure shows the networks of partners for 1995, 2000, 2005, and 2010. Square nodes represent financial firms and circle nodes represent other types of firms. The size of the node represents the degree of the node (how many partners it has). The thickness of the edge represents the value of the contract.

needed to get the money flowing. Figure A1 in the appendix describes the mobility of sponsors across communities in the United Kingdom and the United States.

How is the growth in projects related to the evolution of networks of partners? In the top-ten countries characterized in Tables 1 and 2, these relationships have been positive, with the growth in communities tracking the number of projects. Figure 9 displays these relationships graphically. What is striking is that in the early years of reliance on partnerships for infrastructure, the number of communities exceeds the number of projects, but in most of these

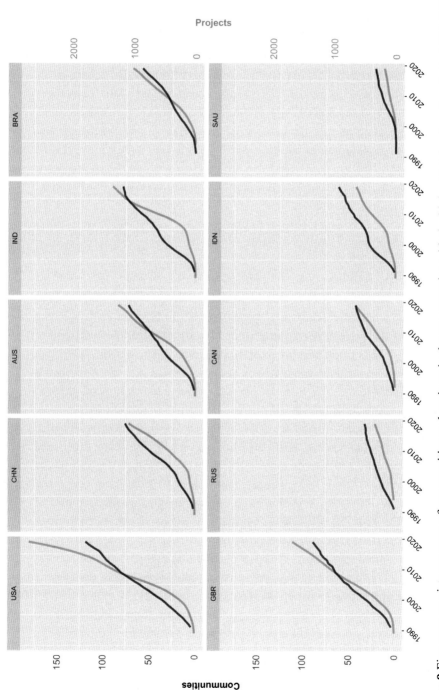

Figure 9 Five-year moving averages of communities and projects in the ten countries with the highest total value of projects, 1985–2020. Black lines denote communities and gray lines indicate total projects. **Source:** Thompson Reuters Securities Data Company.

leading adopter nations, the relationship reverses over time. That is, smaller communities that are disconnected from one another – like the 1995 networks in the northwest quadrants of Figures 7 and 8 – give way to a smaller number of communities that are more interconnected.

Our argument explaining the project announcement–community growth nexus builds on insights about the way firms behave under conditions of uncertainty about production. The seminal contribution of the economists Richard Nelson and Sidney Winter (1982) contends that firms make decisions regarding production on the basis of informal routines and experience, and a long-run equilibrium is not the tendency of markets with a great deal of uncertainty. Routines and experience are developed before the current work of a firm, so the decision-making of firms is, in this sense, backward-looking. These routines can arise when one firm imitates what others in the market are doing or when the firm innovates its own routines. Nelson and Winter (1982) show that different market environments lead to different patterns of imitation or innovation.

Key aspects of the market for partners have characteristics lending themselves to this argument. First, building and operating an infrastructure asset over a long period of time has a large amount of idiosyncratic risk due to the nature of the project, the geography, and, as we examine more directly in Section 4, the political institutions of the country in which the asset is situated. The terms of the PPP contract with the government and the risk-sharing arrangement in the SPV that manages the consortium can protect partners' innovations in the building and operation stage. This allows partners to be more innovative than imitative, in the language of Nelson and Winter (1982). Second, the routines that innovative firms create through their experience must eventually allow for imitation if the use of partnerships for infrastructure is to expand as those in the epistemic community of NPM desire. A useful way to think of this is the transformation of tacit knowledge (the routines of innovative partners) into knowledge that is explicitly transferable to other actors who could create partnerships for infrastructure both within and beyond a nation's borders (Polanyi 1966). We argue that partnership communities play an important role in supporting innovation as well as in transferring knowledge.

Our central claim is that the long-term nature of partnerships for infra-structure with governments allows partnership communities to innovate in particular projects, but the commercial relationships among firms – edges in a national network of partners – protect that innovation by excluding new entrants to the market. Scholars informed by transaction cost economics have argued theoretically and with evidence that relationships become more important in environments of uncertainty (e.g., Crocker and Masten 1991; Crocker and Reynolds 1993). Moreover, management scholars have shown that strategic alliances can reduce coordination cost in such environments (e.g., Artz and Brush 2000). Building on this idea, our claim is that communities reduce project coordination costs – the price of arranging activity to develop a specific asset – and drive the ability of a network of partners to respond to a growing number of projects that a government would like to undertake through partnerships for infrastructure. Thus, we expect that during the initial rise in government demand for partnerships, the number of firms and communities both grow to meet the demand. However, at a point, the market begins to consolidate, as do the British and American networks over time in Figures 6 and 7, respectively. As this happens, new entrants to the network of partners are not excluded, but they face very high coordination costs relative to the members of partnership communities in the consolidating market. As a result, the government does not face a competitive market for partners, but, rather, one in which communities – and the dominant firms, like RBS, within them – hold considerable leverage in forging agreements to build assets.

To evaluate a primary implication of this argument, we test the hypothesis that the number of communities will grow to meet project demand, but only to a point, after which network consolidation will reduce the number of partnership communities even as projects rise. That is, the elasticity (percentage change) of the number of communities in the number of announced projects is positive to a point, but then begins to diminish.

To test this hypothesis, we estimate the elasticities through Poisson regression models with country and year fixed effects. Our dependent variable, *communities* records ln(1 + number of partnership communities). Our primary independent variable, *announced projects*, is calculated as ln(1 + number of announced projects) in the current year. A quadratic specification is employed to estimate the hypothesized drop in elasticity as announced projects increase to a point. To provide evidence that reverse causality is not likely, we also regress the communities metric by a one-year lag of our announced projects measure. The number of communities displays panel serial correlation, so we report standard errors clustered by country.[6]

As Wooldridge (1999, 80–81) shows, the fixed-effects Poisson model does not require a count, but rather, is robust to any distribution of the dependent variable. This is helpful because the announced projects variable (36.28%)

---

[6] Wooldridge tests (Drukker 2003) cannot reject the null hypothesis of no panel serial correlation for communities ($F = 336.85$) or announcements ($F = 1,770.87$).

contains many zero values and the communities measure has a large cluster of cases at its two lowest values (36.75%). We also control for the natural logarithm of national *population* (in millions) and the natural logarithm of real *gross domestic product* (GDP) in millions of constant 2017 US dollars from the Penn World Table, version 10.0 (Feenstra, Inklaar, and Timmer 2015).

Results appear in Table 3. Model 1 reports no statistically significant influence of the number of communities in the prior year on the number of announcements in the current year, providing evidence against reverse causality. Model 2 provides a baseline for our primary claim without the quadratic term, showing that the number of communities is increasing in project announcements. The influence of the quadratic term in Model 3 is negative, as anticipated by our hypothesis.

A portrait of the elasticity of communities in project announcements based on the results of Model 3, shown in Figure 10, provides a clear visual overview of the evidence. The elasticity of communities begins to decline after the annual number of announced projects in a country nears fifty-five. While this supports our hypothesis and provides initial evidence for our argument about network consolidation and community development, we note that the threshold for community consolidation is not high. In 2019, only sixteen countries had less than fifty-five announced projects, as did just 23.3% of all country-year

Table 3 Partnership communities and project announcements, 1985–2020.

Dependent variable	(1) Announced projects (ln)	(2) Communities (ln)	(3) Communities (ln)
Communities (ln)$_{t-1}$	0.038 (0.09)		
Announced projects (ln)$_t$		0.061*** (0.01)	0.383*** (0.06)
Announced projects (ln)$_t^2$			−0.044*** (0.01)
Population (ln)	0.012 (0.04)	−0.005 (0.04)	−0.009 (0.04)
GDP (ln)	0.024 (0.03)	0.181*** (0.04)	0.173*** (0.04)
Constant	0.436 (0.46)	−2.640*** (0.35)	−2.814*** (0.35)
N	3,921	4,093	4,093
Model X^2	81,886.25***	3,890.35***	3,710.13***

Poisson regression models with year and country fixed effects, robust standard errors clustered on the country in parentheses. Significance: * $p < 0.10$, ** $p < 0.05$, *** $p < 0.01$.

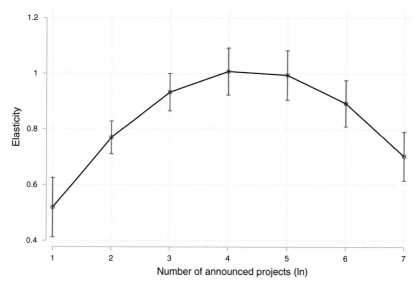

Figure 10 Elasticity of communities in project announcements. Estimates based on Model 3 reported in Table 3. The horizontal axis represents the number of announced projects in the current year (ln).

observations. We hope that scholars will investigate and extend our argument in a variety of ways in the future.

2.7 Conclusion

We began this section by estimating what the networks of partners look like across our global sample. We also operationalized our concept of partnership communities. By comparing the American and British networks of partners, we saw a graphical account of how communities develop over time. Partnership communities give us a new way to see how private firms interact with one another to deliver public infrastructure. In this light, we offered the initial element of our theory of partnership communities, which focused on the changing nature of networks of partners within countries as government demand for partners to build and rehabilitate infrastructure grows. Strong evidence shows that networks begin to consolidate at some point in this growth of demand through the establishment of fewer partnership communities.

Our emphasis now expands on the role of the knowledge of firms and communities in our theoretical argument. In the next section, we construct a metric of project quality that captures which features are associated with the delivery of quality projects, and examine the manner in which these quality projects are situated in countries and in partnership communities.

3 The Quality of Projects

A vibrant element of the literature on public management networks examines their effectiveness in delivering public services (cf. Provan and Milward 1995, 2001; Turrini et al. 2010). In the eyes of government officials seeking to establish partnerships for infrastructure, the ability to turn an announcement into a funded partnership for infrastructure is a crucial step in effective public goods delivery. When private money begins to flow, the political benefits of infrastructure are unlocked, long before the assets under contract begin to produce benefits to citizens. Bertelli (2019) has argued that partnerships for infrastructure have important political benefits for the following reasons. First, they are, in essence, promises to provide public goods, and the benefits of assets are concentrated in voters who use them, while any taxpayer costs associated with the agreement will be paid by a wider group of citizens than those who benefit. Seen prospectively, then, partnerships for infrastructure share characteristics of distributive public policies (cf. Albertus 2013; Weingast and Moran 1983). Second, by involving the private sector through formal contracts, these promises to provide public goods become more credible. Third, the promises are made more valuable through the continuing efforts of governments to get them up and running if and when problems arise. This means that politicians can argue that keeping themselves or their political parties in power is important to unlock the benefits of the assets that will be built through partnerships for infrastructure. Finally, once ground is broken on the asset, it is difficult to redistribute its potential benefits to another group of constituents as a matter of political expediency. For these reasons, the financing of a project has a great deal of political value for incumbent politicians.

Gaining financing for an announced project, in political terms, is a key indicator of the quality of the partners and partnership communities with which a government might work. This argument underlies the measurement task of the current section. As we switch our focus momentarily from partnership communities to the projects and firms within them, we construct a measure of the quality of projects that captures how their characteristics contribute to the likelihood that they will move from the announced to the financed stage. Armed with this measure, we can then bring partnership communities back into our analysis, investigating how network and community features affect the quality of projects. We can then turn our focus in the next section to the crux of our political story, that political institutions shape partnership communities.

3.1 Estimating Project Quality

Our strategy for measuring project quality is based on the approach of Guzman and Stern (2015) to understand the quality of ventures in Silicon Valley. We adopt their approach for characterizing the quality of partnerships, "[r]ather than assume that all ventures have an equal ex ante probability of success, our method allows us to estimate the probability of growth [success] based on information publicly available" (606). The success of a project, seen through our prospective and political lens, is defined as moving a project from the announcement to financing.

3.1.1 Project Quality Indicator

From this definition, we can create regression-based estimates of project quality.[7] Specifically, we identify a number of characteristics that capture the quality of a partnership and regress a binary dependent variable indicating whether project i announced in year t is financed within five years.[8] The unit of analysis is the project-year, and the characteristics of the firms that sponsor the given project are averaged across projects. That is, we estimate a model of the following form via logistic regression:

$$q_{it} = \alpha + \beta p_i + \gamma \bar{f}_t + \eta s_i + \epsilon \tag{1}$$

Here, q_{it} is a binary indicator of whether project i announced in year t is financed within five years of that announcement, p_i is a vector of n characteristics specific to project i, $\bar{f}_t$ is a vector of m characteristics of the sponsoring partners of project i at time t, s_i indicates the sector of project i (e.g., telecommunications).

The partner characteristics variables are constructed to capture recent historical aspects of partnering firms, specifically, over the past five years. Such recent information is most useful to government decision-makers when determining the likelihood that their projects will be financed. Essentially, these "track record" variables relate to the quality of private partners as proxied by their history with partnerships for infrastructure. Our claim is that a partner's track record in terms of project management and delivery is a strong indicator of their quality as a member of a partnership community. Formally, then, for the K firms sponsoring project i, partner characteristic m is defined as $\bar{f}_{mt} = \frac{1}{K} \sum_{k \in K} \sum_{t-5}^{t-1} \frac{f_k}{5}$. In Equation 1, we denote $\sum_m \bar{f}_{mt} = \bar{f}_t$.

Predictions ($\hat{q}_{it}$) from the model in Equation 1 form our measure of the quality of partner i at time t.

---

[7] The distribution of our quality measure is presented in the online appendix, Figure A1.

[8] While the five-year $q_{it} = \alpha + \beta p_i + \gamma \bar{f}_t + \eta s_i + \epsilon$ is included to avoid excluding projects that are funded but which may have lower priority for governments at t, unreported results show that using a contemporaneous measure of financing – namely, indicating that the project is financed in year t – produces robust results and highly correlated predictions.

3.1.2 Observed Project Characteristics

Turning to our measures, two variables capture essential features of the project in question. *Project value* is defined as the monetary value (in millions of US dollars) of the project in question. *Sponsors* records the number of companies sponsoring a given project. Both are indicators of the relative significance of a project in the overall set of partnerships for infrastructure in a given country.

3.1.3 Observed Partnership Characteristics

As noted, partnership characteristics are an average of the sponsor's characteristics and consider a history of five years prior to the announcement of the project in question. As such, all of the following variables (where it is not specified otherwise) are five-year averages.

Announced (count) captures the number of announced projects and *financed (count)* captures the number of financed projects that the sponsors of a project have sponsored.

The remaining variables are derived from the network measures described in Section 2. *Degree* captures the number of commercial relations (network edges) a partner has with other sponsoring partners on a project. *Betweenness* captures the average number of shortest paths on which the sponsor lies (Newman 2018, 173). The foregoing variables capture the extent to which firms have influence within the network of partners of the country in which the project has been announced.

We also include a family of variables that capture the quality of the partnership communities to which the firms sponsoring a project belong. *Community size* measures the average number of firms (nodes) in the community. *Community degree* reflects the average number of connections that members of the community (edges) have had. *Community betweenness* records the average betweenness scores of all sponsors in a given community. We include these variables to capture the influence of partnership communities in helping a project to reach the financed stage.[9]

Finally, we include a bloc of partner fixed characteristic variables that may influence project success. *Financial sponsor* is a binary indicator of whether at least one of the partners on a project is a financial entity, such as a bank. Similarly, *public sponsor* indicates whether a partner is a publicly listed

---

[9] Communities are defined on the basis of network characteristics that evolve over time. We calculate whether a sponsor belongs to a community based on the network structure in any given year, taking into account all of the connections accrued over all of the previous years. This operationalization means that community membership becomes stable over time, as connections between members of a community reinforce themselves. In practice, a sponsor may switch communities upon entrance into the network, but this becomes less likely over time.

company. Financial bodies and publicly listed companies may enjoy higher levels of trust and prestige, making financing more likely for a project.
Descriptive statistics for all of the foregoing variables appear in Table 4.

3.1.4 Estimation

Our measurement modeling proceeds in two stages. From our full sample we select a "model building" subsample comprised of all of the projects for which we directly observe a financing outcome. We run logistic regressions of project, network, and community characteristics on the likelihood of a project being financed within five years. We then use these estimates to calculate the probability of a project being financed given its characteristics for the whole sample. Thus, we create an *ex ante* measure of project quality based on observable characteristics. Formally, the measure is the predicted value from Equation 1:

Table 4 Descriptive statistics.

	Mean	Minimum	Maximum	Standard deviation	N
Year	2009	1990	2020	6.94	26,729
Financed	0.37	0	1	0.48	26,729
Project value (million US $)	936.40	0	214,899.3	3,732.93	21,952
Sponsors	1.73	1	21	1.26	26,729
Public sponsor	0.95	0	13	1.01	26,729
Financial sponsor	0.13	0	7	0.40	26,729
Announced (count)	2.8	0	66	5.58	26,729
Financed (count)	1.19	0	48	2.84	26,729
Degree	1.99	0	70.6	4.95	26,729
Betweenness	446.56	0	59,268.37	2,554.67	26,729
Community size	9.32	0	288	23.79	26,729
Community degree	1.2	0	17.69	2.13	26,729
Community betweenness	124.74	0	5,522.8	422.31	26,729

Table 5 Logistic regression estimates for the measurement model of project quality, odds ratios.

	Odds Ratios			
	Model 1	Model 2	Model 3	Model 4
Project value	0.999***	0.999***	0.999***	0.999***
	(0.000)	(0.000)	(0.000)	(0.000)
Sponsors	1.068***	1.069***	1.029	1.028
	(−0.020)	(−0.020)	(−0.020)	(−0.020)
Announced (count)	0.920***	0.918***	0.917***	0.919***
	(−0.007)	(−0.007)	(−0.008)	(−0.007)
Financed (count)	1.219***	1.211***	1.218***	1.216***
	(−0.018)	(−0.018)	(−0.019)	(−0.018)
Degree	0.979**	0.982*	0.983*	0.983*
	(−0.007)	(−0.007)	(−0.008)	(−0.008)
Betweenness	1.000	1.000	1.000	1.000
	(0.000)	(0.000)	(0.000)	(0.000)
Community size	1.001	1.001	1.001	1.001
	(−0.001)	(−0.001)	(−0.001)	(−0.001)
Community degree	1.053***	1.057***	1.061***	1.061***
	(−0.015)	(−0.015)	(−0.015)	(−0.015)
Community betweenness	1.000	1.000	1.000	1.000
	(0.000)	(0.000)	(0.000)	(0.000)
Public sponsor	1.114***	1.122***	1.104***	1.108***
	(−0.025)	(−0.026)	(−0.026)	(−0.026)
Financial sponsor	1.398***	1.372***	1.382***	1.378***
	(−0.062)	(−0.061)	(−0.062)	(−0.062)
Sector fixed effect	No	Yes	Yes	Yes
Year fixed effect	No	No	Yes	Yes
Number of observations	16,902	16,902	16,902	16,902
Log likelihood	−10,815.005	−10,715.897	−10,588.863	−10,627.303
Deviance	21,630.010	21,431.794	21,177.726	21,254.605
AIC	21,654.010	21,475.794	21,271.726	21,304.605
BIC	21,746.832	21,645.968	21,635.280	21,497.985

The dependent variable is project financed (=1). Significance: *** $p < 0.001$; ** $p < 0.01$; * $p. < 0.05$. Robust standard errors reported in parentheses. Model 4 includes a spline function for the year variable.[12]

---

[12] Coefficients expressed as probabilities are reported in the online appendix, Table A4. As a robustness test, we replicate these models and include non-lagged versions of the independent variables. Results are presented in Tables A5 (odds ratios) and A6 (probabilities) of the online appendix. We also replicate Model 4, changing the duration of the lag from five years to various other intervals to demonstrate that our results do not depend on the five-year period (Table A7). Our results are robust to all aforementioned tests.

$$\hat{q}_{it} = P(q_{it} = 1 \mid p_i, \bar{f}_t, s_i) = F\left(+\beta p_i + \gamma \bar{f}_{i,t} + \eta s_i\right).^{10}$$

3.1.5 Results

Our main specification includes fixed effects so as to address unobserved hetero-geneity within years and sectors. We do not include country fixed effects, following Guzman and Stern (2015), so as to remain agnostic about the quality of projects from a given location. Model 1 in Table 5 is our full specification, which includes the explanatory variables described earlier, but without fixed effects for sector and year. These explanatory variables can be observed by the government and all partners upon the announcement of the project because they capture recent historical attributes of the firms as well as the project itself. Model 2 includes sector fixed effects, while Model 3 includes both sector and year fixed effects, but we cannot use this model for prediction as our model building sample and our predicting sample do not fully overlap in years. To correct for this, Model 4 includes standard sector fixed effects and semiparametric year fixed effects (B-spline). This allows us to include the *year* variable in our predictions whereas this would not be possible if using *year* as a factor variable because of the lack of overlap in years across the samples we have noted. For these reasons, we interpret Model 4 subsequently.[11] Models 1–4 are strikingly robust in the factor effects that they uncover, both in size and significance.

Project value is negatively associated with the likelihood of financing, although the effect size is small: for every additional US\$1 million, the likeli-hood of a project being financed decreases by just 0.04%. By comparison, looking at *sponsors*, an additional partner sponsoring a project is not a significant factor in predicting success.

Partners' recent history of involvement in partnerships for infrastructure is also predictive of success. For each additional *announced* project in a partner's recent portfolio, the likelihood of a project being financed decreases by 8.49%. Being associated with one additional *financed* project correlates with an increase in the likelihood of success of a substantial 19.52%. *Degree* (*p value* = 5% and the effect size is very small) and partner *betweenness* are not significant factors in predicting success.

---

[10] We disregard projects announced prior to 1990 as they are few and distributed unequally across countries.

[11] Faced with the choice between using sector fixed effects only (Model 2) or double (sector: standard fixed effect, year: semiparametric fixed effect) fixed effects (Model 4), we prefer the fuller model that also has a lower Akaike information criterion (Akaike 2011).

Community size and *community betweenness* are not significant factors in predicting success. *Community degree* is positively correlated with the likelihood of a project being financed, where *ceteris paribus*, if a community has just one more commercial relationship, on average, the project is 5.92% more likely to be financed.

For every additional *public sponsor* among a project's sponsors, a project is 10.26% more likely to achieve financing. Finally, for every additional *financial sponsor*, a project is 32.04% more likely to achieve financing.

3.2 Project Quality across Countries and Time

Aggregating our predictions from Model 2 to the country level provides a picture of the geographical distribution of the quality of projects across the globe. Figure 11 shows average project quality $(\hat{q}_{it})$ between 1990 and 2020 across the countries in our sample.

One striking feature is that the map tracks the spread of NPM, with high-quality projects developing across the thirty years of the movement in countries such as the United Kingdom, United States, Japan, and New Zealand. The adoption of NPM by development banks has spread the demand for quality projects to Africa, Central and South America, and South Asia. The evolution of project quality in this spirit is more clearly seen in Video 1, which shows the early concentration of quality projects in Western Europe and North America, followed by their spread through Eastern Europe and the developing world.[13]

Figure 11 also provides some heartening face validity for our quality metric. For instance, the Indonesian province of Papua has a much lower quality score than the adjacent commonwealth nation of Papua New Guinea. Likewise, the partner quality in Thailand is significantly greater than bordering and less developed Myanmar.

Figure 12 shows the relationship between the number of projects in a country and their quality. Some countries such as the United Kingdom and United States have large numbers of partnerships for infrastructure, but also maintain high project quality. Controlling for sector and year, quantity and quality are positively correlated,[14] a high average quality for projects can be found in Slovenia and Japan (with the highest average project quality scores), France, Sweden, and Switzerland, despite their smaller numbers. Looking at specific sectors is also illuminating. For example, the modal sector in the United States is wind energy, it has a very high number of projects and a high quality score. By

---

[13] Section 4 of the appendix reports movies of the evolution of announced and financed projects, by nation, for the years 1990–2020.

[14] A linear model regressing quality on the number of projects in a country with sector and year fixed effects shows a coefficient of 0.25 ($p < 0.01$, $N = 21,950$, overall $R^2 = 0.66$).

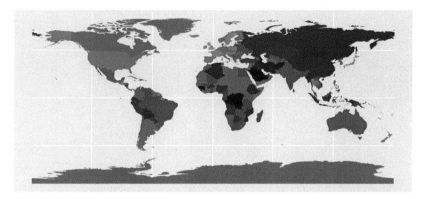

Video 1 Evolution of average quality measures aggregated at the country level over time, 1990–2020. Video showing annual changes in the average quality measures. Countries are colored by average quality centile. Lighter colors correspond to higher centiles. Countries with fewer than ten projects are not included. Video available at www.cambridge.org/partnershipcommunities

contrast, China's modal sector is hydroelectric power, and it has a relatively high number of projects, but a lower quality score.

3.3 Conclusion

This section introduced a method for measuring the quality of projects and illustrated the measure across countries and time. The measure is based on a pre-construction indicator of project success – the probability that a project announced by the government is financed by a consortium of partners. This is a critical phase for the political argument we advance in the next section, as financing allows politicians to truly unlock the benefits of partnerships for infrastructure. The likelihood of success is significantly impacted by project value and the number of partners in the consortium, but also by characteristics of the national partnership communities that lie at the center of our argument. These models can be used to produce a metric of project quality that is crucial for understanding the role of political institutions in partnerships for infrastructure.

4 Political Institutions, Project Quality, and Community Development

Political institutions – the rules of the game in a nation's politics – have profound impacts on business arrangements. Political economists see the reason for this as related to the question of whose preferences matter in shaping the formal and informal rules of economic activity (cf. Acemoglu, Johnson, and Robinson 2001; Accmoglu and Robinson 2006; North 1990). Economic institutions, such as the

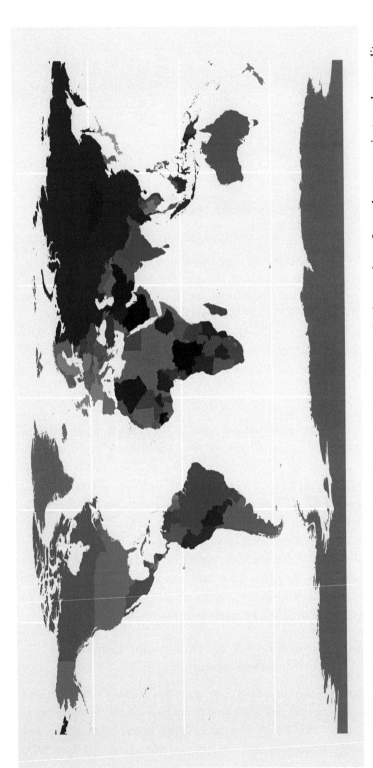

Figure 11 Average partner quality across countries and time, 1990–2020. Countries in gray have fewer than ten projects and no quality measure is calculated. Lighter colors represent higher quality.

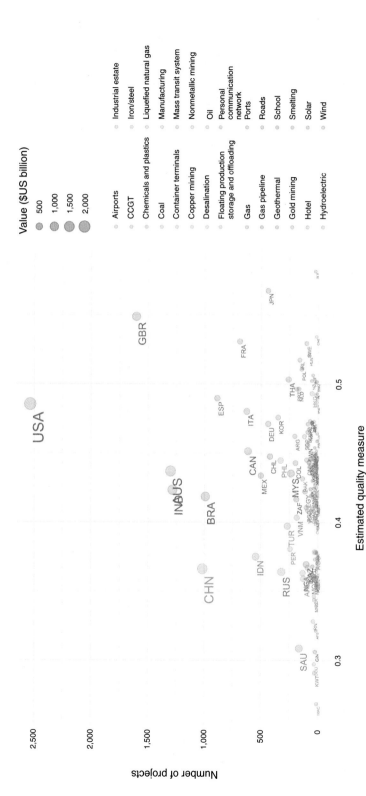

Figure 12 Quantity versus quality in partnerships for infrastructure, 1990–2020. The vertical axis shows the total number of projects and the horizontal axis reflects our estimates of project quality. The size of the bubbles represent the total value of partnerships for infrastructure in a given country from 1990 to 2020, while the color represents the modal sector in which projects are concentrated.

contractual arrangements of partnerships for infrastructure, build the economy, but they also distribute resources across groups in the polity, which makes them important to its politics. While the distribution of resources across groups influences the real political power of the groups in society – the "haves" have more power than the "have nots" – formal political institutions provide formal authority to make political choices about the distribution of resources and the rights of individuals and groups to determine them (Acemoglu and Robinson 2006).

Our argument is centered on the notion of credible commitments. The importance of political institutions in our present context is due to their commitment value – that is, the extent to which they give business actors credible beliefs that politics functions in a certain way (Bertelli and Whitford 2009). The rule of law has also enhanced commitments, and with them economic activity, for centuries. Adherence to law and the acceptance of judicial decisions gives business an expectation of fair treatment in courts when disputes arise (cf. Haggard, MacIntyre, and Tiede 2008, 211; Milgrom, North, and Weingast 1990). When commitments are more credible, the political-economic environment is more predictable.

In this section, we examine the commitment value of political institutions and the rule of law in shaping the quality of projects and the character of partnership communities. The key to understanding communities, we claim, comes not through the discipline that competitive elections place on politicians (Adserà, Boix, and Payne 2003), but in the uncertainty partners face about the policy leanings of and their personal relationships with government officials (Bertelli 2019; Gehlbach and Keefer 2012; Henisz 2000; Lobina 2005). When institutions help partners to mitigate uncertainty, quality is enhanced and partnership communities are strengthened. Political and legal institutions translate uncertainty into risk, and that risk can be managed through the development of partnership communities. How configurations of institutions reduce uncertainty is a nuanced question. Sometimes, institutions and norms we might see in a negative light do a better job in reducing uncertainty because they created more predictable behavior than the instruments of "good governance." We present and empirically evaluate an argument that captures some of the complexity of the relationship between institutions and uncertainty in the context of partnerships for infrastructure.

4.1 Democracy, the Rule of Law, Project Quality, and Communities

To establish a conceptual language for the argument that follows, we consider two key characteristics of partnership communities in this section: their size and the connectedness of actors within them. As explained in Section 2, the size of these communities can be understood as the number of nodes within them. We can capture the connectedness of partnership communities with two metrics that were discussed earlier. Degree reveals number of commercial relationships that members of a community have, while betweenness indicates how likely it is for a partner to be located on a path between two others in a community. The former represents the extent of collaboration within the community, while the latter indicates the extent to which communities are important in financing and implementing partnerships for infrastructure. In the argument that follows, we say that *stronger* partnership communities are larger and more connected – that is, their actors both substantially collaborate with one another (higher degree) and are more involved in the business of their communities (higher betweenness).

4.1.1 Democracy

Many quantitative studies focus on a minimal definition of democracy – namely, that elections are competitive (Cheibub, Gandhi, and Vreeland 2010) – while others take a more expansive view of democracy's requirements (Coppedge et al. 2017). To understand whether electoral competition influences partnerships for infrastructure, we begin with the minimal approach. Following Boix, Miller, and Rosato (2013), we focus on two aspects of what Dahl (1971) calls polyarchy: participation and contestation. Democracies are those nations in which political participation is based on "a minimal level of suffrage" and where "the decisions to govern the state are taken through voting procedures that are free and fair" (Boix, Miller, and Rosato 2013, 1527). In this way, the influence of democracy on government–business relationships like PPPs might emerge from the ability of citizens to hold governments to account in elections.

While we understand that democracy is correlated with good governance and economic growth, we argue that it is not unequivocally attractive to investment and helpful to the success of partnerships. The potential instability of the interests and policies of a government partner in a partnership for infrastructure as a result of competitive elections and accountability can create uncertainty that lowers project quality and increases the risks to partners. As we have argued throughout, partnership communities develop as a response to the need for risk sharing, and these risk-sharing networks are more likely to participate in projects in democratic countries. While we will argue momentarily that the reason *why* democracies have these effects on quality and partners is more nuanced than the ability of citizens to hold governments to account – that it depends on a crucial characteristic of national party systems – we test this relationship as a threshold claim.

Hypothesis 1: Political systems satisfying minimal levels of participation and contestation are associated with lower average project quality and stronger partnership communities.

4.1.2 The Rule of Law

The rule of law provides investors with confidence that contractual commitments will be backed up by the judicial system, and it is positively correlated with democratic institutions (e.g., Adserà, Boix, and Payne 2003).[15] Haggard, MacIntyre, and Tiede (2008, 207) wrote, "[s]ome trade can take place in the form of barter or exchanges in which transactions clear immediately, but more complex transactions require the ability to make and receive promises about future actions. This is particularly true of financial transactions, which, from a legal point of view, are primarily contracts." PPPs are tremendously complex arrangements involving government actors, and they are constituted of contracts. Adherence to the rule of law makes commitments stronger, which allows partners to invest in the production of high-quality projects. It also makes projects more appealing from an investment standpoint, which strengthens partnership communities. As with democracy, we think that the influence of the rule of law is more nuanced, but we begin by testing the following claim.

Hypothesis 2: Nations that adhere to the rule of law are associated with higher average project quality and stronger partnership communities.

4.1.3 Opposition Parties and the Government

We contend that one element of political contestation that is crucial to project quality and the strength of partnership communities lies in the party system. Kam, Bertelli, and Held (2020) argue with evidence from twenty-eight parliamentary democracies that electoral accountability – the possibility that government parties will be turned out – is stronger when government and opposition parties form ideologically distinct blocs. Quite straightforwardly, this distinctiveness gives the voter the ability to discern how to sanction the government by voting for an opposition party.

When opposition parties are distinct from those in government, they generate risks for partners. Because it seems to suggest that a healthier democracy is worse for governance, this may seem counterintuitive, but it becomes clearer when we recognize that functioning democratic institutions have both risks and

---

[15] The polyserial correlation between the Boix, Miller, and Rosato (2013) binary indicator of democracy and the World Bank's continuous measure employed subsequently, which explicitly references contract enforcement, is 0.66.

stabilizing tendencies. Risks come from the possibility that competitive elections will change the partisan and ideological composition of the government, and thereby create the possibility that government preferences about the project and partnerships for infrastructure more generally may change with it. The independence of opposition and government parties lies at the core of our argument, and we test the following hypothesis.

Hypothesis 3: When opposition parties enjoy independence from government parties, project quality is lower and partnership communities are stronger.

4.1.4 Judicial Corruption

As with democracy, we argue that the rule of law influences project quality and community strength in a subtle way. We argue that corruption in the judicial system is a crucial consideration for partners. Specifically, where corruption undermines partners' confidence that they can resolve disputes through the courts, they "are forced back on the costly alternative of private enforcement, and investment and trade suffer accordingly" (Haggard, MacIntyre, and Tiede 2008, 211). Given the complexity of PPPs as a matter of contract, and the fact that the government is itself a party to the contracts in question, private enforcement is not a likely option for resolving contractual contingencies. PPPs are by definition long-term arrangements, which are, in turn, part formal contracts and part informal relationships with the members of partnership communities, particularly the dominant members. As in any complex contracting environment in the public domain, the management of relationships with a partnership community is crucial to the ability of the government to sustain its "credibility with the pool of potential and existing contractors as well as the citizens on whose behalf the contracted tasks are performed" (Bertelli and Smith 2010, i28). While the latter is a problem for electoral accountability as influenced by the party system through the claim we test as Hypothesis 1, the former is a concern for the rule of law. A judicial system in which bribes or side payments are common undermines its credibility with the members of a partnership community. While this argument compels no expectation about its impact on project quality, we test the following hypothesis.

Hypothesis 4: When bribes are common in connection with judicial proceedings, partnership communities are weaker.

4.1.5 Bureaucratic Corruption

Corruption in the public sector more broadly is somewhat different in character. A large literature is inconclusive on how corruption influences economic growth. While influential theoretical arguments suggest that corruption raises costs through rent-seeking behavior (e.g., Bhagwati 1982), in one meta-analysis of 460 estimates of the relationship between corruption and growth, 6% are positive, 32% are negative, and 62% are statistically insignificant (Campos, Dimova, and Saleh 2010). An alternative argument is that public-sector corruption can help highly productive firms efficiently negotiate burdensome administrative procedures (Leff 1964), although the evidence for this claim is not particularly strong (Aidt 2009).

Returning to the role of uncertainty that lies at the center of our argument, we argue that bureaucratic corruption allows better quality projects to emerge because side payments can reduce the arbitrary application of administrative rules. However, we expect that the cost of this corruption comes in the character of the communities that emerge, which are smaller and have fewer mutual commercial arrangements among them, but with partners that are more tightly linked. In this way, the partnership communities in contexts of corrupt public administration provide a less competitive environment for governments when they launch PPPs. We test the following hypothesis.

Hypothesis 5: Bureaucratic corruption is associated with higher-quality projects and smaller partnership communities with a lower degree.

4.1.6 Particularistic Social and Infrastructure Spending

The political systems in some countries have a strong tradition of providing public goods broadly, while others have a penchant for targeting these goods toward particular groups of constituents. We expect that the latter tradition, with its incentives for pork-barreling or distributive politics, has an influence on the quality of projects and the character of partnership communities. Bertelli (2019) argues that even the *ex ante* promise of infrastructure through PPP projects – quite apart from whether they are delivered – allows politicians to claim credit for targeted public goods. Woodhouse (2019) shows some evidence that these *ex ante* incentives do shape the distribution of projects across the political geography of a large number of countries. We argue that a particularistic tradition for public goods provision is associated with lower-quality projects, and with stronger communities. Lower-quality projects are incentivized because of the importance of *ex ante* credit claiming, while stronger communities – larger, greater degree, and more betweenness – are the result of the popularity of these projects with politicians who demand infrastructure project launches for electoral purposes.

Hypothesis 6: A tradition of particularistic public goods provision is associated with lower-quality projects and stronger partnership communities.

4.1.7 Residual Claims to Infrastructure Assets

Some types of PPP agreements, such as a build-operate-transfer agreement, leave government a residual claim to the assets that are built by partnerships for infrastructure – that is, when the operating contract is finished, the government becomes the owner of the asset and can contract for its operation with anyone it chooses. This eventual ownership stands in contrast with other arrangements, such as the BOO agreement that we observed in Section 3 to be the modal type of PPP in our data. Here, the government has no residual claim to the asset, which remains the property of the consortium at the end of the long-term PPP arrangement.

When government has a residual claim, it can rightly view the asset as more public, even though its commitment to private involvement is long-term. Bertelli (2019) argues that the claim to publicness makes a project with a residual government claim to the asset being constructed more politically valuable and therefore more salient with incumbent politicians. We contend that the higher salience of projects with residual government claims improve their quality, and that the risks attendant to this higher political attention invite the participation of partnership communities that are larger and better connected. We test the following hypothesis.

Hypothesis 7: Projects in which the government has a residual claim to the asset are of higher quality and are associated with stronger partnership communities.

4.2 Data and Methods

To test our hypotheses, we estimate two sets of statistical models. First, we estimate models to assess the influence of broader concepts of minimal democracy and the rule of law on project quality and the strength of partnership communities (Hypotheses 1 and 2). Second, we examine the influence of particular institutional features (Hypotheses 3–7) through more specific measures based on elite surveys. We estimate these models separately due to the sizeable correlations between the broader conceptual measures of democracy and the rule of law with the more specific institutional measures.[16] The unit of analysis in each of the statistical models that follow is the project.

---

[16] For instance, the correlation between the democracy and opposition party autonomy measures is 0.81, while the correlation between the rule of law and the judicial and public sector corruption measures are both 0.93.

4.2.1 Concept Models

We begin with an initial investigation of the role of democracy and the rule of law on partnership communities. Our dependent variables are the measure of *project quality* (mean = 0.36, SD = 0.13) established in the last section as well as the average *community size* (mean = 9.89, SD = 25.24), *community degree* (mean = 2.00, SD = 2.71), and *community betweenness* (mean = 181.97, SD = 495.90) described in Section 2. Our quality measure represents the conditional probability of an announced project being financed given the project and firm characteristics discussed in the last section. Community size represents the average number of nodes (partners), community degree represents the average number of edges that connect a node, and community betweenness the average betweenness metric[17] for the communities involved with a project.

To examine the influence of a minimal conception of democracy (Hypothesis 1), we employ the Boix, Miller, and Rosato (2013) measures of democracy and regime duration, which were sourced from the Quality of Government Standard Dataset (Teorell et al. 2020). *Democracy* (mean = 0.82, SD = 0.38) is a binary indicator of a country's compliance with the Boix, Miller, and Rosato (2013) definition of democracy in the year recorded. To understand the influence of the *rule of law* in a broad sense (Hypothesis 2), we use a measure drawn from the World Bank's Worldwide Governance Indicators project (Kaufmann, Kraay, and Mastruzzi 2010). This aggregate measure combines objective information and survey responses to capture "perceptions of the extent to which agents have confidence in and abide by the rules of society, and *in particular the quality of contract enforcement*, property rights, the police, and the courts, as well as the likelihood of crime and violence" (Kaufmann, Kraay, and Mastruzzi 2010, 4, emphasis added). The availability of these models restricts our sample to a smaller number of observations (17,283) than in the models testing our additional hypotheses.

We include several control variables in our concept models. A binary indicator of projects announced within the *first five years* (mean = 0.11, SD = 0.32) of the history of partnerships in our data set captures unmeasured attributes of an initial period of learning about this form of governance. The natural logarithm of the *project cost* in US dollars (mean = 4.71, SD = 2.50) controls for issues arising from the size of projects. We also include controls for population and the size of the economy through the natural logarithms of national *population* in millions of persons (mean = 4.28, SD = 1.60) and real *GDP* in millions of 2017 US dollars (mean = 14.17, SD = 1.70) from the Penn World Table, version 10.0 (Feenstra, Inklaar, and Timmer 2015).

---

[17] Specifically, we calculate vertex (node) betweenness, which is the number of shortest paths on which a vertex lies.

4.2.2 Institutions Models

The Varieties of Democracy (V-Dem) project (Coppedge et al. 2021) provides several elite survey-based measures that can be employed to test Hypotheses 3–7, while our primary data set provides a measure for testing Hypothesis 8. The time coverage of the V-Dem measures allows us to examine a larger sample of projects (25,522) than in the democracy and rule-of-law models. Our dependent variables are once again *project quality* (mean = 0.40, SD = 0.15), *community size* (mean = 9.48, SD = 24.10), *community degree* (mean = 1.90, SD = 2.65), and *community betweenness* (mean = 216.28, SD = 639.12).

While the underlying response sets for the V-Dem survey questions are ordinal, we use the interval measures that result from the measurement model employed by the project team to make comparisons across countries easier to justify (Coppedge et al. 2021). The V-Dem variable names appear in parentheses with their summary statistics for our preferred specification. To examine Hypothesis 3, we measure *opposition party autonomy* (v2psoppaut, mean = 1.87, SD = 1.41) that captures whether opposition parties – those not in government – are independent of the parties in government (Coppedge et al. 2021). To test Hypothesis 5, we include a measure of *judicial corruption* (v2jucorrdc, mean = 1.10, SD = 1.41) that takes higher values when bribes and side payments are frequently made to hasten judicial decision-making. A measure of *public-sector corruption* (v2excrptps, mean = 0.88, SD = 1.43) is used to examine Hypothesis 6. This variable takes higher values if it becomes more likely that bureaucrats give favorable treatment in exchange for bribes and side payments. The importance of *public goods* spending (v2dlencmps, mean = 1.25, SD = 0.78) is at the heart of the claim in Hypothesis 7, and we examine this with a variable that takes lower values as social and infrastructure spending is generally more targeted toward specific groups of constituents, but higher values as the these spending categories are intended to benefit all constituents, for example, subject to means testing.

Finally, to test Hypothesis 8, we include a binary indicator of a PPP project in which there is a *government residual claim* (mean = 0.14, SD = 0.34) to the asset.[18] We include the same control variables as in our democracy and rule-of-law models: *first five years* (mean = 0.14, SD = 0.35), *project cost* (mean = 4.54, SD = 2.52), *GDP* (mean = 14.22, SD = 1.69), and *population* (mean = 4.31, SD = 1.55).

We estimate all of our linear models via ordinary least squares regression. Our strategy for identifying the hypothesized effects is to include country and project

---

[18] This indicates that the SDC data record the project as a build-lease-transfer (N = 97), build-operate-transfer (N = 796), build-own-operate-lease-transfer (N=27), build-own-operate-maintain-transfer (N = 27), build-own-operate-sell (N = 4), build-own-operate-transfer (N = 234), build-own-transfer (N = 67), build-transfer-operate (N = 64), design-build-operate-transfer (N = 111), lease-refurbish-operate-transfer (N=25), or rehabilitate-lease-transfer (N = 14).

sector fixed effects. We exploit within-year variation, while controlling for unobserved heterogeneity within project sectors (e.g., wind energy) and countries. We also estimate standard errors clustered on the country-sector-year triad to address unmodeled heterogeneity specific to sectors within a country in a particular year.

4.3 Results

The results of our concept models appear in Table 6. Hypotheses 1 and 2 expect that the democracy and rule-of-law measures, respectively, would be positive and significant across all models. Strikingly, Hypothesis 1 is soundly rejected as a threshold explanation. Our estimates reveal no influence of a minimal level of democracy on either project quality or the strength of partnership communities. The contract-relevant rule-of-law measure, by contrast, is associated with higher project quality. In Model 2,[19] *ceteris paribus*, a 10% stronger perception of the rule of law is associated with a 1.3% increase in project quality. The only other statistically significant relationship emerges in the base model of community betweenness (Table 6, column 7), but this effect is not robust to the inclusion of the control variables. Overall, this evidence suggests that a more contoured portrait of political and judicial institutions is necessary to understand their impact on project quality and community strength.

Our controls prove influential for each dependent variable. Greater project cost and GDP both negatively impact project quality. The project cost effect on community size, degree, and betweenness is also positive and statistically significant. Population, by contrast, reaches statistical significance at the 0.05 level only in Model 8, where it is associated with greater betweenness centrality in partnership communities.

The results of our institutions models are presented in Table 7. Hypothesis H3 anticipates negative effects of the opposition party autonomy variable in the quality models, but positive coefficients in the size, degree, and betweenness models. This is precisely what we observe. In Model 2, all else equal, a 10% increase in opposition party independence from government parties corresponds to a 1.8% decrease in project quality. A 10% increase in opposition party independence in Model 4 corresponds to a 2.3% increase in the number of firms in a community, a 2.2% increase in community degree and a 4.8% increase in community betweenness when other variables are held at their means.

The influence of a corrupt judiciary conforms to Hypothesis 2. While it has no influence on project quality, judicial corruption reduces the size, degree, and betweenness centrality of partnership communities. Holding all other variables at

---

[19] As we discuss results, we will interpret our preferred specifications, which include the control variables mentioned earlier.

Table 6 The influence of democracy and the rule of law on project quality and partnership communities.

	Quality		Community size		Community degree		Community betweenness	
Democracy (= 1)	−0.013	−0.012	−1.197	−1.580	−0.155	−0.193	12.907	3.450
	(0.020)	(0.018)	(1.043)	(1.007)	(0.253)	(0.241)	(20.505)	(19.396)
Rule of law	0.060***	0.085***	2.358	2.093	0.182	0.350	88.416***	46.390
	(0.014)	(0.013)	(1.924)	(1.891)	(0.256)	(0.251)	(34.149)	(31.532)
First five years (= 1)		0.040***		−2.850***		−0.442***		−3.654
		(0.005)		(0.866)		(0.089)		(14.612)
Project cost (ln)		−0.009***		0.395***		0.117***		13.093***
		(0.001)		(0.090)		(0.010)		(2.118)
GDP (ln)		−0.103***		−0.263		−1.309***		70.277**
		(0.012)		(1.614)		(0.242)		(32.060)
Population (ln)		0.005		6.751		0.975*		471.318***
		(0.026)		(4.921)		(0.528)		(100.840)
Constant	0.335***	1.800***	9.443***	−16.771	2.016***	15.817***	118.340***	−2921.899***
	(0.015)	(0.145)	(1.286)	(29.794)	(0.238)	(2.439)	(22.598)	(564.209)
N	17,336	17,283	17,336	17,283	17,336	17,283	17,336	17,283
R^2	0.35	0.40	0.16	0.16	0.15	0.17	0.20	0.21

Linear models incorporate country and sector fixed effects. Robust standard errors clustered on the country-sector-year unit in parentheses. Significance: * $p < 0.10$, ** $p < 0.05$, *** $p < 0.01$.

Table 7 The influence of accountability and party ideology on project quality and partnership communities.

	Quality		Community size		Community degree		Community betweenness	
Opposition party autonomy	-0.034***	-0.037***	1.310***	1.152**	0.259***	0.224***	72.432***	55.418**
	(0.006)	(0.006)	(0.507)	(0.550)	(0.073)	(0.075)	(23.769)	(23.870)
Judicial corruption	-0.012	0.003	-0.998	-1.408*	-0.524***	-0.385***	-52.945**	-82.537***
	(0.007)	(0.007)	(0.755)	(0.806)	(0.101)	(0.105)	(25.146)	(30.298)
Public-sector corruption	0.021***	0.039***	-1.361	-1.244	-0.261**	-0.056	89.280***	90.996***
	(0.007)	(0.007)	(1.181)	(1.309)	(0.114)	(0.109)	(26.532)	(26.181)
Particular public goods	-0.062***	-0.050***	3.593***	3.461***	0.248***	0.242**	83.428***	94.278***
	(0.006)	(0.006)	(0.793)	(0.817)	(0.096)	(0.097)	(21.081)	(21.907)
Government residual claim	0.021***	0.013***	0.646	0.788	0.545***	0.462***	-9.572	5.012
	(0.003)	(0.003)	(0.659)	(0.664)	(0.069)	(0.068)	(13.101)	(12.674)
First five years (= 1)		0.105***		-3.109***		-0.177**		10.430
		(0.005)		(0.743)		(0.075)		(24.925)
Project cost (ln)		-0.010***		0.302***		0.096***		9.702***
		(0.000)		(0.086)		(0.009)		(3.333)
GDP (ln)		-0.078***		-1.384		-0.969***		-22.027
		(0.011)		(1.127)		(0.173)		(28.499)

Population (ln)		0.122***		7.104		0.259		1,003.496***
		(0.032)		(5.482)		(0.481)		(152.538)
Constant	0.531***	1.110***	4.674***	−6.411	1.812***	13.833***	−41.162	−4,055.312***
	(0.012)	(0.117)	(1.007)	(15.346)	(0.150)	(1.572)	(42.584)	(745.731)
N	26,000	25,522	26,000	25,522	26,000	25,522	26,000	25,522
R^2	0.31	0.40	0.14	0.15	0.14	0.16	0.18	0.20

Linear models incorporate fixed effects for country and sector. Robust standard errors clustered on the country-sector-year unit in parentheses. Significance:
* $p < 0.10$, ** $p < 0.05$, *** $p. < 0.01$.

their mean values, a 10% increase in judicial corruption is associated with decreases of 1.6% in the size, 2.1% in the degree, and 4.0% in the betweenness centrality of partnership communities.

The expectation of Hypothesis 5 is that public-sector corruption corresponds to higher-quality projects, but lower degree and betweenness centrality in partnership communities. This claim is supported in regard to quality and betweenness, but not for degree. *Ceteris paribus*, a 10% increase in our public-sector corruption measure is associated with a quite small 0.8% increase in quality. While a negative relationship with degree is reported in Model 5 at the $p = 0.05$ levels in all models in Table 7. Other variables at their means, a 10% increase in particularism relates to a 1.5% decrease in project quality and to increases of 4.6% in community size, 1.6% in degree, and 5.5% in betweenness centrality.

Our final hypothesis (Hypothesis 7) expects that when the government has a residual claim to an asset, as when it takes ownership after the consortium completes construction, project quality is higher and community size, degree, and betweenness are larger. The claim is partially supported by our estimates, although the effects are small and limited to quality (Models 1 and 2) and degree (Models 5 and 6). All else at mean levels, a government residual claim corresponds to a small increase in quality of less than one-tenth of a standard deviation. The impact of a residual claim on community degree in Model 6 is an increase of 17.5% of a standard deviation, *ceteris paribus*.

As in the concept models, our control variables have explanatory power in the institutions models. The first five years of PPP experience is associated with higher project quality (Model 2) but smaller communities (Model 4) with lower degree (Model 6). As project cost rises, quality falls (Model 2), while the size (Model 4), degree (Model 6), and betweenness centrality (Model 8) of communities all rise. Higher levels of GDP are associated with lower project quality (Model 2) and lesser degree in communities (Model 6). Finally, larger countries are associated with higher-quality projects (Model 2) and partnership communities with greater betweenness centrality (Model 8).

4.4 Conclusion

This section presents our theory of the influence of political and judicial institutions on the quality of projects and the size and connectedness of the partnership communities involved in them. The results of our statistical models reveal that in a large sample of projects over the past thirty years, our argument is generally supported.

We argued that the minimal requirements of many empirical studies of democracy are not sufficient to understand the influence of representative governments, likewise with the rule of law. Threshold analyses in our concept models suggest that while perceptions that the rule of law is followed in a country are associated with higher-quality projects, a minimal conception of democracy that focuses on participation and contestation (Boix, Miller, and Rosato 2013) is not statistically associated with either quality or any of the characteristics of partnership communities we study.

Drilling down on both concepts reveals subtleties in the way that political and legal instructions influence both quality and communities. We argue that one important effect of representative government comes from the nature of the party system in a country. Risks to partners arise from potential changes in the partisan and ideological composition of the government because political engagement with and support of PPPs may be altered. We find that when opposition parties are independent from those in government parties – a logical premise for such shifts – project quality is reduced and communities are strengthened. This suggests that while the risk associated with government commitment to projects relates to lower quality, the partnership communities associated with those projects are stronger and have the potential to buffer the downside of that risk.

Corruption in the judiciary and bureaucracy have quite different effects on project quality and partnership communities. Judicial systems that frequently involve side payments for efficient processing and favorable outcomes weaken partnership communities, but do not influence quality. While the rule of law and quality are in harmony, judicial corruption is associated with weaker communities and potentially with a lower ability for government to establish partnerships for infrastructure. Bureaucratic corruption appears to improve the quality of projects and the betweenness centrality of partners within communities. We think that while side payments can reduce the unpredictability of bureaucratic application of rules to projects, the tighter linkage of partners buffers risk by reducing competition among potential partners. This has efficiency implications that must be sorted out by future research.

The distributive character of infrastructure projects is also an important factor for understanding quality and community characteristics. A tradition of pork-barrel politics in social and infrastructure spending weakens project quality, but a residual claim for the government, which enhances the credit politicians can claim for launching it, enhances quality. The presence of distributive politics generally strengthens partnership communities as well.

Our findings are important in that they shed light on how formal political and judicial institutions shape relationships between business actors and governing politicians, specifically the degree to which business actors believe that they can predict the types of behaviors that they can expect from a government. By developing a measure of the quality of projects and modeling the communities that produce such projects, we are able to go below a surface-level understanding that looks only at the number of partnerships produced and pays minimal attention to the configurations of actors that produce such projects. This marks a significant step toward understanding the political economy of partnerships, something that has been missing from the literature to date.

That said, there are several areas in which there is room for direct improvement of our analyses. For example, given our global focus in this study, we purposefully had to choose a limited set of universally observable measures of the quality of partnerships for infrastructure in order for the measure to be applicable across countries. By focusing on a smaller geographic region, future work could sharpen such a measure and drill down into which dimensions of quality are most affected by political institutions, for instance, projects that are more durable, accessible, profit-making, or environmentally friendly. Similarly, our measures could be enriched with more information about the companies involved in the partnerships for infrastructure that we studied – capturing characteristics about them outside the projects themselves to include such observables as their value, the composition of their boards, and the geographic scope of their operations.

Future work should also seek to directly measure the risk faced by business actors. Some risks are quantifiable and observable, for example, by codifying the contracts that companies enter into with governments and the financial risk that they bear as a formal matter. Others are perceived and can be gleaned through interviews with key members of partnership communities to understand their perceptions of different types of governments and how that affects firms willingness to enter into business with them.

Community detection is an emerging field and we expect this approach and techniques to advance significantly over the coming years, which we hope will enhance our understanding of partnership communities. Additional research along these lines may shed light on the importance of the small, but significant, effects of political institutions on the size and connectedness of partnership communities.

Finally, our argument and evidence leave an important question unstudied: Do voters care whether infrastructure is provided through PPPs? If voters trust these arrangements, politicians have an even greater incentive to rely on them. But if there is something about partnerships for infrastructure that concerns voters, then the incentives to use them could be diminished. We turn to this question in the following section, uncovering an important mechanism that links voter decision-making to the institutional influences we have been discussing.

5 Voters, Accountability, and the Structure of Partnerships

In the previous section, we reported evidence that the institutional foundations of policy commitments play a role in shaping both the quality of projects and the size and connectedness of the partnership communities involved in them. In this section, we shift our unit of analysis and turn our focus toward voters. We do this because we still lack a clear understanding of the effect that different modes of infrastructure delivery might have on how voters attribute responsibility for public goods and how they change their preferences over incumbent politicians. Here we investigate whether and how different arrangements in infrastructure development affect voters' preferences toward the incumbent. We do this by situating some experimental results from a larger project in the United States (Woodhouse, Belardinelli, and Bertelli 2021) to address a crucial question: Do voters care whether infrastructure is provided through PPPs?

5.1 Infrastructure and Distributive Politics

We begin from the premise that voters are more likely to be interested in the mechanisms for providing public goods and services if they can or do benefit from those goods or services. Distributive policies consist of political decisions that concentrate benefits – in the form of infrastructure, water treatment centers, land reclamation, and so on – in a specific geographic constituency and finance expenditures through generalized taxation (Weingast, Shepsle, and Johnsen 1981). A second premise is that the interest of voters must have the potential to influence their vote for incumbent politicians, leading them to strategically distribute public goods and services. In building an inventory of studies on distributive politics, Golden and Min (2013) find that those focused on democratic accountability conceptualize distributive allocations as attempts by politicians to protect themselves electorally by targeting specific groups of voters. In a nutshell, a reelection-seeking incumbent can target distributive public goods – for example, a road or a water treatment facility – toward voters who will benefit, and, crucially, whose votes the politician needs for political survival (e.g., Thomas Bohlken 2019). The nature of the exchange of targetable goods for electoral payoff can vary (Cox 2010). For example, benefits can be given to voters before they vote, or they can be promised upon the victory of a relevant candidate or party.

An emerging line of studies in public administration and political science considers how distributive patterns differ according to the nature of the public good itself (cf. Albertus 2013; Bertelli 2019). What is more, Woodhouse (2019) provides cross-national evidence that partnerships for infrastructure are used as distributive goods to target swing districts. She argues that the manner in which they are distributed depends upon the credit-claiming opportunity presented by the partnership. What we know very little about is how voters respond to targeted assets created or refurbished through partnerships.

5.2 Citizen Perspectives on Partnerships for Infrastructure

Our theory in the previous section relies on the retrospective sanctioning perspective of electoral accountability. This means that voters have greater power to reject, *ex post*, a government that they do not want because of policy performance or anything else, than to select, *ex ante*, a government they do want on the basis of promised policies (Kam, Bertelli, and Held 2020; Manin 1997). This includes the possibility that infrastructure projects might be considered by voters as a reason to reject incumbent parties at the ballot box. That is, in voters' judgments about the costs and benefits of public projects and the way these projects (from which they might benefit) are delivered to citizens might play a role.

Partnerships for infrastructure allow governments to provide public goods that are valuable beyond a single payment by leveraging private investments and risk-sharing (Hodge and Greve 2007). They represent a form of public-service delivery that falls between the two extremes of state provision, full public management, and market provision, full private management (cf. Delmon 2011; Hodge and Greve 2011). On the one hand, in partnerships in which government has a residual claim to an asset, the asset itself might be viewed as more public. Bertelli (2019) argues that the claim to publicness makes such projects more politically valuable and therefore more salient to incumbent politicians. If voters associate a publicly, but not a privately, managed asset with the actions of politicians, infrastructure delivered through a partnership rather than full public or private management will increase their willingness to vote for the incumbent politician. This logic informs the following hypothesis.

Hypothesis 9: Voters will be more likely to express an intention to vote for an incumbent politician responsible for infrastructure delivered through a partnership than for infrastructure delivered through full private management.

On the other hand, behavioral public administration studies point to the existence of "anti-public sector bias" (Marvel 2015a). These studies emphasize that individuals' behavior, both within and outside public organizations, is often inconsistent with neoclassical economic models that depict individuals as perfectly rational decision-makers. Human beings are, rather, endowed with bounded rationality (Simon 1956), meaning partial knowledge and limited computational skills, and they are affected by cognitive biases preventing them from consistently revealing their preferences (Khaneman 2002). Cognitive biases result from individuals' tendency to rely on simple heuristics that reduce the complexity of each decision to simpler judgmental operations (Artinger et al. 2015; Gigerenzer and Todd 1999; Kahneman 2011). A recent review of cognitive biases in public administration studies (Battaglio et al. 2019) shows that an anti–public-sector bias affecting individuals' attitudes toward government organizations has been widely reported in the literature (Christensen et al. 2018; Hvidman and Andersen 2015; Marvel 2015a, 2015b). On this view, repeated exposure to anti–public-sector messages would bias citizens' evaluation of public-sector organizations' performance. In particular, citizens would automatically see public-sector organizations as less efficient than their private counterparts (Marvel 2015a). If this is the case, infrastructure delivered through a partnership, compared to infrastructure delivered through full public management, will increase voters' willingness to vote for the incumbent politician. This behavioral argument admits a second hypothesis:

Hypothesis 10: Voters will be more likely to express an intention to vote for an incumbent politician responsible for infrastructure delivered through a partnership than for infrastructure delivered through full public management.

Of course, the realized quality and performance of projects might very well contribute to shaping voters' preferences. Bridges may be clogged with traffic, and tolls too high. The crisp, clean water from a new facility may lead voters to recycle their plastic bottles of spring water for the last time, or allow an underserved community reliable access to potable water for the first time. What we expect is that *ceteris paribus* – that is, keeping performance levels fixed, expectations regarding how different modes of infrastructure delivery affect voting intentions should impact their evaluations of the incumbents who want credit for the benefits these assets bring to voters.

5.3 Survey Experiment

We designed a survey experiment to investigate the effect of different arrangements of infrastructure delivery on voters' preferences (e.g., Belardinelli et al. 2018). Our sample was constituted of 1,194 adults in the United States, with responses gathered through invitations sent to the Qualtrics research panel in July 2019. Based on national estimates from the Current Population Survey (Census QuickFacts), we established sampling quotas for region, sex, age, and race.[20] In our experimental scenario, participants are first asked to imagine that their congressional representative has won funding for a project in their district. The project is either a toll road or a water treatment center, depending on the randomly assigned condition. After being given a provisional expected time needed to complete the construction phase (in particular, they know that the project will be ready for use in two years), respondents are provided with information about the mode of public-service delivery, which is our main manipulation. Participants were randomly assigned to one of three different experimental conditions. One group read that the government is in charge of the construction of the project and the government is in charge of the management of the project for the next twenty years, once it has been constructed. A second group read that a private company is in charge of the construction of the project and a private company is in charge of the management of the project for the next twenty years, once it has been constructed. A third read that the government is in charge of the construction of the project and a private company is in charge of the management of the project for the next twenty years, once it has been constructed. Having been informed about the project, participants were then asked to indicate their voting intention regarding the incumbent member of the United States Congress (Woodhouse, Belardinelli, and Bertelli 2021). Once respondents revealed their preferences on these outcomes, we asked them to imagine that the project has been realized, so that they now know the actual time needed in order to complete the construction phase. Two different times for completing construction were given by random assignment: either two years (as planned) or four years (two more than planned). Subsequently, respondents were again asked to indicate their voting intention regarding the incumbent (Woodhouse, Belardinelli, and Bertelli 2021).

Table 8 reports treatments and treatment levels of the experiment, and additional descriptive information appears in the online appendix.

To capture vote intention, subjects were asked to indicate, on a scale from 0 to 100, how likely they would be to vote for the representative of their district in the next congressional election. We asked this question both before and after subjects are informed about the time frame for the completion of the construction phase of the project. In addition, once respondents have indicated their likelihood to vote for the representative, we ask them to explain their choice.

A series of comparison of means tests reveal that, as a consequence of the randomization process, experimental groups did not differ across demographic

---

[20] A full description of the experimental design and details related to participants in this experiment are included in Woodhouse, Belardinelli, and Bertelli (2021).

Table 8 Treatments and treatment levels of the experiment.

Treatment	Levels
Mode of infrastructure delivery (construction phase/management phase)	- Fully private (private/private) - Fully public (government/government) - PPP (government/private)
Performance of the construction phase	- Two years (as planned) - Four years (two more than planned)
Type of project	- Toll road - Water treatment center

characteristics. Results from a linear probability model further show that before performance information about the construction phase is released, a hybrid mode of infrastructure delivery in the form of a partnership for infrastructure increases the probability of supporting the incumbent with respect to both full public management and full private management.

Figure 13 shows the proportion of subjects who are more likely to express intention to support the incumbent, by mode of infrastructure delivery. *Ceteris paribus*, the probability of expressing intention to support the incumbent decreases by seven percentage points ($p = 0.05$) when full public management is adopted and by four percentage points ($p = 0.20$) when full private management is adopted, rather than a partnership.

Before performance information is released, citizens shape their views according to the actors involved in the delivery process. In particular, with no performance information available about projects, Hypotheses 9 and 10 are both confirmed, as voters show a preference for projects delivered through partnerships, compared to both full public and full private management. This preference toward a hybrid form of infrastructure delivery is also observed in responses to an open-ended question following the experimental block, which asked "[w]hat features of the project influenced your [vote intention] rating, or simply what was your gut reaction to the information you read?" Respondents offered the following: "Regardless of how effective the project is, it is still a good concept to support ... I approve of partnering with the private sector and them paying the costs," "the government controls it private individuals manage at [sic] ... As long as they are doing a good job things are working well with the government and the private sector and it's beneficial to the citizens the process should work hopefully." Aversion toward both fully private or public provision is also clear from some of the open-ended

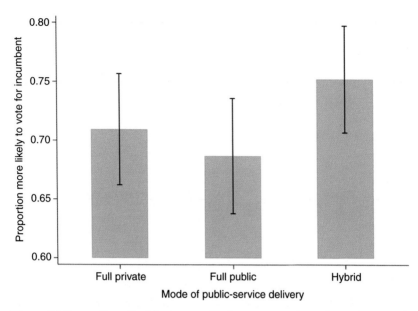

Figure 13 Proportion of subjects more likely to express intention to support the incumbent by mode of infrastructure delivery before performance information about construction is released.

responses. Some respondents show their skepticism toward the private sector: "public works projects should be owned and operated by the people (government) not privatized," "Private companies cheat the public!!!," "I am just not a fan of these privately run toll roads," "Private companies are usually no good." Other respondents show their distrust and disappointment toward government provision: "The government cannot do anything correctly the government is useless," "I don't trust government. They make promises they can't deliver," "Government projects [sic] typically over budget and late," "Nothing run by the government is done efficiently or at a cost that is worth what is done," "Anytime government is involved in running something it seems like bad things can and do happen," "the fact the government is running it, it is sure to fail" (Woodhouse, Belardinelli, and Bertelli 2021).

Nonetheless, some respondents seem to anticipate the fact that performance information would make a difference in shaping their voting intention: "it depends how the project goes," "would want to see how project evolves," "the project must be finished first," "would like to see projects completed." Indeed, after performance information about the construction phase is released, participants seem to be less concerned about the form of delivery and to pay more attention to performance in infrastructure delivery. Incumbent vote intention does not differ depending on the mode of delivery, as shown in Figure 14. By contrast, participants exposed to the late construction (two years more than planned) were less likely to express intention to support the incumbent (by 25 percentage points, $p < 0.001$), with respect to participants exposed to a construction phase that was completed on time (Figure 15).

Our experiment reveals partial support for the claims in Hypotheses 1 and 2. Before encountering performance information, voters seem to prefer infrastructure delivery through partnerships, rather than relying exclusively on the government or a private entity. When voters do know about project performance, they become indifferent to the mode of delivery. Importantly, the observed pattern of results holds across different types of project. While, on average, the toll road project, compared to the water treatment center, elicited significantly lower incumbent support, the effects of different modes of delivery and of different performance levels of the construction phase do not differ between the toll road project and the water treatment center.

5.4 Conclusion

Results from this survey experiment suggest that partnerships might be more effective than public or private provision for politicians wanting to enhance vote

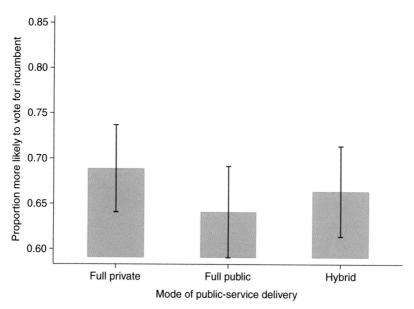

Figure 14 Proportion of subjects more likely to express intention to support the incumbent, by mode of infrastructure delivery after performance information about construction is released.

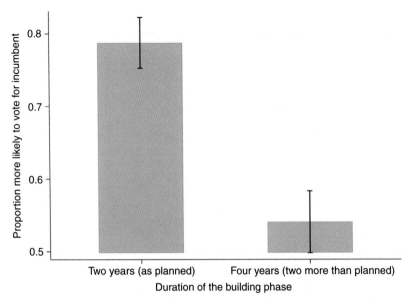

Figure 15 Proportion of subjects more likely to express intention to support the incumbent by performance of the first phase after performance information about construction is released.

share from infrastructure provision. But our evidence also suggests that this effect only exists before the project is completed and voters can assess its performance. Once the infrastructure is in place, voters are concerned only about the performance of service delivery, regardless of the actors involved. These results present the first evidence about the impact of partnerships for infrastructure on vote intention to our knowledge.

What we have found, of course, should be interpreted in light of the limitations affecting experimental designs, especially in terms of external validity. We hope that future research will test these results against alternative units, treatments, and contexts. One interesting test might be to replicate the experiment in different countries. Variation in performance information should also be considered, for instance, quality of services to target populations rather than delays in completion. Moreover, a variety research methods should be used to explore a host of related questions. How do citizens view partnerships as a specific mechanism for providing public goods? Are they aware of their potential? Are they personally aware of their performance and connection to political action? Qualitative methods in particular might illuminate these types of questions. Focusing inquiry on politicians, rather than voters, would be useful in order to dig deeper into credit-claiming strategies and how these relate to alternative arrangements of infrastructure delivery. While our study shows that there is some potential for using partnerships as an aid in claiming credit for infrastructure before it starts performing its function, a direct test would require a focus on politicians' behavior.

6 Implications of Partnership Communities for Theory and Practice

We have systematically investigated the role of partnership communities in infrastructure development around the world for the first time. While the overwhelming focus of the literature on partnerships for infrastructure has been on individual projects, we analyze how the private firms involved in partnerships for infrastructure are interconnected, globally and domestically. And we show the influence of democratic institutions and the accountability of incumbent politicians in shaping the nature of these communities and the quality of the projects they sponsor. The result is a new portrait of a widely used hybrid governance structure.

In Section 1, we defined partnership communities as networked communities of private firms that form the consortia that enter into long-term contractual arrangements with governments. They stand between hierarchy and markets, between power and prices. Their competitive advantage lies in their ability to respond to a growing number of projects that a government would like to undertake through partnerships and in reducing the transaction costs of coordination. In Section 2, we argued and showed how, within countries, partnership communities are affected by government demand for partners in infrastructure development. We made the case that, during the initial rise in government demand for partnerships the number of firms and communities both grow to meet demand and at some point networks begin to consolidate. Even though new firms continue to enter the network, they face very high coordination costs relative to the members of partnership communities in the consolidating market. Section 3 introduced a novel measure of project quality, given by the probability that a project announced by the government is financed by a consortium of partners. Strikingly, we showed that the higher the project value, the lower the likelihood of successful financing. This finding is echoed in Section 4 (Table 7), where project value was also found to be negatively correlated with project quality. By contrast, the number of partners in the consortium seems to be positively associated with the likelihood of success. Moreover, we report significant variation across space and time, by showing how different national partnership communities have followed divergent paths in recent history. Interestingly, the spread of high-quality projects seems to track the spread of NPM across the globe.

What is more important is that our measure of project quality allows us to investigate how quality is affected by national institutions. In Section 4, we showed that a political party system in which opposition parties enjoy independence is associated with lower-quality projects but stronger communities to mitigate the risk of a change in partisan composition of the government. While perceptions of a functioning rule of law correspond to higher-quality projects, partnership communities are weaker where courts routinely accept bribes. Yet our evidence is consistent with the claim that side payments to bureaucrats can make rule application less certain and project quality higher, but partnership communities where this is common seem more tightly linked to mitigate the risks such a system produces. Systems in which distributive politics is strong in infrastructure and social spending see lower project quality but stronger partnership communities. Moreover, when political credit-claiming is heightened by the presence of a government residual claim, the quality of projects is higher. Political and judicial institutions have important influences on partnerships for infrastructure and the communities of partners who produce them.

Section 5 delves deeper into electoral dynamics by changing the unit of analysis and investigates whether and how voters' preferences toward incumbent politicians are affected by the mode of infrastructure delivery. A survey experiment on a representative sample from the United States reveals that voters reward incumbent politicians for partnerships for infrastructure, compared to state or market provision. In other words, partnerships might be the most effective way for politicians to engage in *ex ante* credit-claiming for infrastructure (Bertelli 2019).[21] Still, this effect only exists before the project is completed. Once in place, voters are concerned only about an asset's performance, regardless of the actors involved in its financing and delivery.

Our study offers a few main lessons for scholars and practitioners alike. Partnerships for infrastructure are a powerful tool because they allow for the "bundling" of construction and management such that a single consortium of private partners bears the risks for both phases (Engel, Fischer, and Galetovic 2014). As infrastructure is one of the fundamental ingredients for competitive industries (Porter 1990), practitioners should pay careful attention to their national partnership communities and can manage financing and delivery given the reality that they are not facing a competitive market. While quite a lot of evidence exists on the conditions that can render partnerships more or less suitable to deliver infrastructure, to the best of our knowledge, ours is the first attempt to understand how partnership *communities* can make infrastructure projects better. For example, the size of partnership communities, as

---

[21] See note 16.

measured by the number of partners involved in the consortium, seems to make announced projects more likely to be financed. Our data reveal that an infrastructure project with at least one financial body among its sponsors is more likely to achieve financing. The same holds for projects with at least one publicly listed company among its sponsors. These might become important variables for public managers and policymakers when evaluating partnership communities. The intense focus on value for money in the literature and media coverage of partnerships for infrastructure seems to mask these considerations, which also have important managerial implications for firms that must weigh the benefits and costs of involvement in a partnership community.

Our findings uncover questions that are ripe for future research. To take but one example, why might it be that including publicly listed companies improves the chances of attracting funds? There are a wide range of mechanisms that might be investigated. Public bodies might contribute in different ways to the consortium. On the one hand, they might provide additional and updated knowledge for more evidence-based projects that are, therefore, more likely to succeed. On the other hand, their main role in the partnership community might be to increase the credibility of the project through their reputation. These mechanisms might also apply to research bodies.

There is much work that remains to be done in terms of strengthening the theoretical groundwork for and description of partnership communities. For example, research exploring the types of firms involved in partnership communities would be extremely valuable in terms of both describing how the sectoral composition of communities changes over time and of understanding whether alliances emerge between certain sectors as communities establish themselves. As we briefly illustrated with the RBS example in Section 2, by looking in more detail at the types of firms involved in partnership communities and who they form alliances with, one can start to understand some of the phenomena that shape the political and commercial environment in which partnerships are embedded. This could open avenues of research that shed light on how and why different sectors may use partnerships to varying degrees to deliver goods and services, in addition to the more traditional explanations relating to the complexity of projects and national governments' available financing options.

Practitioners should be very aware of the risks involved in high-value projects, which seems to be associated with a lower likelihood of success. Future research should unpack this correlation, and investigate more deeply the factors that can make specific partnership communities better or worse partners for government on specific infrastructure projects. Similarly, it would be important to explore whether the same conclusions can be drawn depending on the national context and, for example, on whether and to what extent an

NPM-style approach may have replaced the traditional model of public management within a country.

Both politicians and practitioners should understand that when they announce projects for potential financing, they do not only get financing in return. They stimulate the development of partnership communities, which can make or break their projects and become a reliable or fleeting source of funds for infrastructure development. They may have some market features, but they are not the features envisioned by many champions of NPM (cf. Bertelli, Mele, and Whitford 2020; Hood 1991; Lynn 1998). While our emphasis has been on national communities, the phenomenon is global and the partners are networked globally. Future scholarship should investigate these connections more clearly, but current policymakers cannot ignore it.

A second interesting implication is that the characteristics of political and judicial institutions make partnership communities more or less successful in attracting funding for projects. Our argument and evidence suggest that particular characteristics of these institutions might well trigger the creation of weaker partnership communities and this might also result in the delivery of lower-quality projects. This raises significant concerns about the ability of partnerships for infrastructure to create public value (e.g., Bryson, Crosby, and Bloomberg 2014). Our experimental data in Section 5 suggest that performance seems to be what voters value most when thinking of infrastructure projects. Where electoral accountability is weak, practitioners might want to make an effort in trying to create alternative incentives to monitor long-term projects. Monitoring may require important mechanisms of stakeholder participation. More fully collaborative arrangements, with stakeholders involved in meaningful deliberation and decision-making with the consortium of partners and state actors (e.g., Ansell 2011; Bertelli, McCann, and Travaglini 2019), could temper the influence of the electoral incentives we have uncovered. Future research can dig deeper into which dimensions of quality are most affected by political institutions.

Our analysis of voters' preferences also has an important implication. One might be led to think that trade-offs between politicians' short-term goals and projects' performance are being made in the context of partnerships for infrastructure. If our results say anything, it is that, at least in the short term, voters are sensitive to the mode of delivery and that they might be well inclined to electorally reward an incumbent politician who might be responsible for infrastructure projects delivered through partnerships. This means that politicians might try to exploit this sensitivity in order to maximize electoral outcomes at the expense of project performance. Indeed, in each specific infrastructure project, it is not necessarily the case that the mode of delivery preferred by voters before a project is carried out will be the one capable of delivering the highest level of performance once the project is ready for use. If this is not the case, voters will be penalized by lower performance in the long term. Future research should explore further these dynamics, which speak to electoral accountability mechanisms by introducing the possibility that voters ask for what they do not really want – that is, relaxing rationality as a constraint on their choices. Moreover, studies in this vein should examine the ways in which established and emerging partnership communities, and the dominant firms within them, influence voters' decisions about accountability for their representatives. Such a behavioral perspective might be particularly fruitfully applied when considering voters' forward-looking concerns, which is different from our retrospective sanctioning perspective of electoral accountability and in which uncertainty and behavioral biases might play a major role.

To conclude, we believe that this study will help the public administration community to start thinking about partnership communities as important organizations for infrastructure development. We have shown the importance of taking these communities into consideration when studying infrastructure, by shedding light on their structure and performance, their impact upon the delivery of quality projects, and how they can be shaped by political institutions. We hope the theory and evidence in this study will trigger further rigorous research on partnership communities that will benefit scholars and practitioners alike through a deeper, more nuanced understanding of the constellations of actors involved in the delivery of our public goods.

References

Acemoglu, Daron, Simon Johnson, and James A. Robinson. 2001. "The Colonial Origins of Comparative Development: An Empirical Investigation." *American Economic Review* 91(5): 1369–1401. doi: 10.1257/aer.91.5.1369.

Acemoglu, Daron, and James A. Robinson. 2006. *Economic Origins of Dictatorships and Democracy.* New York: Cambridge University Press. doi: 10.1017/CBO9780511510809.

Adserà, Alícia, Carles Boix, and Mark Payne. 2003. "Are You Being Served? Political Accountability and Quality of Government." *Journal of Law, Economics, and Organization* 19(2): 445–490. doi: 10.1093/jleo/19.2.445.

Aidt, Toke S. 2009. "Corruption, Institutions, and Economic Development." *Oxford Review of Economic Policy* 25(2): 271–291.

Akaike, Hirotugu. 2011. "Akaike's Information Criterion." In *International Encyclopedia of Statistical Science*, ed. Miodrag Lovric. New York: Springer. doi: 10.1007/978-3-642-04898-2_110.

Albertus, Michael. 2013. "Vote Buying with Multiple Distributive Goods." *Comparative Political Studies* 46(9): 1082–1111. doi: 10.1177/0010414012463897.

Angulo Amaya, Maria Camila, Anthony Michael Bertelli, and Eleanor Florence Woodhouse. 2020. "The Political Cost of Public–Private Partnerships: Theory and Evidence from Colombian Infrastructure Development." *Governance* 33(4): 771–788. doi: 10.1111/gove.12443.

Ansell, Christopher. 2011. *Pragmatist Democracy: Evolutionary Learning as Public Philosophy.* New York: Oxford University Press.

Artinger, Florian, Malte Petersen, Gerd Gigerenzer, and Jürgen Weibler. 2015. "Heuristics as Adaptive Decision Strategies in Management." *Journal of Organizational Behavior* 36(S1): S33–S52. doi: 10.1002/job.1950.

Artz, Kendall W., and Thomas H. Brush. 2000. "Asset Specificity, Uncertainty and Relational Norms: An Examination of Coordination Costs in Collaborative Strategic Alliances." *Journal of Economic Behavior and Organization* 41(4): 337–362. doi: 10.1016/S0167-2681(99)00080-3.

Bajari, Patrick, Stephanie Houghton, and Steven Tadelis. 2014. "Bidding for Incomplete Contracts: An Empirical Analysis of Adaptation Costs." *American Economic Review* 104(4): 1288–1319. doi: 10.1257/aer.104.4.1288.

Bajari, Patrick, Robert McMillan, and Steven Tadelis. 2009. "Auctions versus Negotiations in Procurement: An Empirical Analysis." *Journal of Law, Economics, and Organization* 25(2): 372–399. doi: 10.1093/jleo/ewn002.

Ball, Rob, Maryanne Heafey, and David King. 2001. "Private Finance Initiative: A Good Deal for the Public Purse or a Drain on Future Generations?" *Policy and Politics* 29(1): 95–108. doi: 10.1332/0305573012501224.

Battaglio Jr., Paul R., Paolo Belardinelli, Nicola Bellé, and Paola Cantarelli. 2019. "Behavioral Public Administration *ad fontes*: A Synthesis of Research on Bounded Rationality, Cognitive Biases, and Nudging in Public Organizations." *Public Administration Review* 79(3): 304–320. doi: 10.1111/puar.12994.

Belardinelli, Paolo, Nicola Bellé, Mariafrancesca Sicilia, and Ileana Steccolini. 2018. "Framing Effects under Different Uses of Performance Information: An Experimental Study on Public Managers." *Public Administration Review* 78(6): 841–851. doi: 10.1111/puar.12969.

Bertelli, Anthony M. 2019. "Public Goods, Private Partnerships, and Political Institutions." *Journal of Public Administration Research and Theory* 29 (1): 67–83. doi: 10.1093/jopart/muy036.

Bertelli, Anthony Michael, Pamela J. Clouser McCann, and Giulia Leila Travaglini. 2019. "Delegation, Collaborative Governance, and Nondistributive Policy: The Curious Case of Joint Partnerships in American Federalism." *Journal of Politics* 81(1): 377–384.

Bertelli, Anthony M., Valentina Mele, and Andrew B. Whitford. 2020. "When New Public Management Fails: Infrastructure Public–Private Partnerships and Political Constraints in Developing and Transitional Economies." *Governance* 33(3): 477–493. doi: 10.1111/gove.12428.

Bertelli, Anthony M., Valentina Mele, and Eleanor Florence Woodhouse. 2020. "Corruption, Democracy, and Privately Financed Infrastructure." *Administration and Society* 53(3): 327–352. doi: 10.1177/0095399720944548.

Bertelli, Anthony M., and Craig R. Smith. 2010. "Relational Contracting and Network Management." *Journal of Public Administration Research and Theory* 20(suppl. 1): i21–i40.

Bertelli, Anthony M., and Andrew B. Whitford. 2009. "Perceiving Credible Commitments: How Independent Regulators Shape Elite Perceptions of Regulatory Quality." *British Journal of Political Science* 39(3): 517–537. doi: 10.1017/S0007123409000623.

Bhagwati, Jagdish N. (1982). "Directly Unproductive Profit-Seeking (DUP) Activities," *Journal of Political Economy* 90: 988–1002.

Binz-Scharf, Maria Christina, David Lazer, and Ines Mergel. 2012. "Searching for Answers: Networks of Practice among Public Administrators." *American Review of Public Administration* 42(2): 202–225. doi: 10.1177/0275074011398956.

Blondel, Vincent, Jean-Loup Guillaume, Renaud Lambiotte, and Etienne Lefebvre. 2008. "Fast Unfolding of Communities in Large Networks." *Journal of Statistical Mechanics: Theory and Experiment* (10): P10008.

Boix, Carles, Michael Miller, and Sebastian Rosato. 2013. "A Complete Data Set of Political Regimes, 1800–2007." *Comparative Political Studies* 46 (12): 1523–1554. doi: 10.1177/0010414012463905.

Bryson, John M., Barbara C. Crosby, and Laura Bloomberg. 2014. "Public Value Governance: Moving beyond Traditional Public Administration and the New Public Management." *Public Administration Review* 74(4): 445–456. doi: 10.1111/puar.12238.

Campos, Nauro F., Ralitza D. Dimova and Ahmad Saleh. 2010. "Whither Corruption? A Quantitative Survey of the Literature on Corruption and Growth." IZA Discussion Paper No. 5334. https://ssrn.com/abstract= 1716129.

Carrillo, Patricia, Herbert Robinson, Peter Foale, Chimay Anumba, and Dino Bouchlaghem. 2008. "Participation, Barriers, and Opportunities in PFI: The United Kingdom Experience." *Journal of Management in Engineering* 24(3): 138–145. doi: 10.1061/(ASCE)0742-597X(2008) 24:3(138).

Cece, Fiona. 2020. "Navigating the Conceptual Discrepancies of Public–Private Partnerships in Literature and in the Field: What Constitutes a Public–Private Partnership?" Dissertation, Bocconi University.

Cheibub, José Antonio, Jennifer Gandhi, and James Raymond Vreeland. 2010. "Democracy and Dictatorship Revisited." *Public Choice* 143(1): 67–101. doi: 10.1007/s11127-009-9491-2.

Chen, Cheng, Michael Hubbard, and Chun-Sung Liao. 2013. "When Public–Private Partnerships Fail: Analyzing Citizen Engagement in Public–Private Partnerships: Cases from Taiwan and China." *Public Management Review* 15(6): 839–857. doi: 10.1080/ 14719037.2012.698856.

Christensen, Julian, Casper M. Dahlmann, Asbjørn H. Mathiasen, Donald Moynihan, and Niels B. G. Petersen. 2018. "How Do Elected Officials Evaluate Performance? Goal Preferences, Governance Preferences, and the Process of Goal Reprioritization." *Journal of Public Administration Research and Theory* 28(2): 197–211. doi: 10.1093/jopart/ muy001.

Coppedge, Michael, John Gerring, Staffan I. Lindberg, et al. 2017. "V-Dem Methodology v6." Methodology Project V6. March 2016. doi: 10.2139/ ssrn.2951040.

Coppedge, Michael, John Gerring, Carl Henrik Knutsen, et alet al. 2021. "V-Dem Codebook v11.1" Varieties of Democracy (V-Dem) Project. www .v-dem.net/en/data/reference-material-v11/

Coviello, Decio, and Mario Mariniello. 2014. "Publicity Requirements in Public Procurement: Evidence from a Regression Discontinuity Design." *Journal of Public Economics* 109: 76–100. doi: 10.1016/j.jpubeco.2013 .10.008.

Cox, Gary W. 2010. "Swing Voters, Vore Voters, and Distributive Politics." In *Political Representation*, eds. Ian Shapiro, Susan C. Stokes, Elisabeth Jean Wood, and Alexander S. Kirshner, Cambridge: Cambridge University Press, 342–357. doi: 10.1017/CBO9780511813146.015.

Crocker, Keith J., and Scott E. Masten. 1991. "Pretia Ex Machina? Prices and Process in Long-Term Contracts." *The Journal of Law and Economics* 34 (1): 69–99. doi: 10.1086/467219.

Crocker, Keith J., and Kenneth J. Reynolds. 1993. "The Efficiency of Incomplete Contracts: An Empirical Analysis of Air Force Engine Procurement." *The Rand Journal of Economics* 24(1): 126–146. doi: 10.2307/2555956.

Dahl, Robert A. 1971. *Polyarchy: Participation and Opposition*. New Haven, CT: Yale University Press.

Delmon, Jeffrey. 2011. *Public–Private Partnership Projects in Infrastructure: An Essential Guide for Policy Makers*. Cambridge: Cambridge University Press. doi: 10.1017/9781108163729.

de Silva, Dakshina G., Timothy Dunne, Anuruddha Kankanamge, and Georgia Kosmopoulou. 2008. "The Impact of Public Information on Bidding in Highway Procurement Auctions." *European Economic Review* 52(1): 150–181. doi: 10.1016/j.euroecorev.2007.07.003.

Drukker, David M. 2003. "Testing for Serial Correlation in Linear Panel-Data Models." *The Stata Journal* 3(2): 168–177. doi: 10.1177/1536867X0300 300206.

Engel, Eduardo, Ronald D. Fischer, and Alexander Galetovic. 2014. *The Economics of Public–Private Partnerships: A Basic Guide*. New York: Cambridge University Press.

Feenstra, Robert C., Robert Inklaar, and Marcel P. Timmer. 2015. "The Next Generation of the Penn World Table" *American Economic Review* 105 (10): 3150–3182.

Forrer, John, James Edwin Kee, Kathryn E. Newcomer, and Eric Boyer. 2010. "Public–Private Partnerships and the Public Accountability Question." *Public*

Administration Review 70(3): 475–484. doi: 10.1111/j.1540-6210.2010.02161.x.

Freeman, Linton, Douglas Roeder, and Robert Mulholland. 1979. "Centrality in Social Networks: II. Experimental Results." *Social Networks* 2(2): 119–141. doi: 10.1016/0378-8733(79)90002-9.

Gehlbach, Scott, and Philip Keefer. 2012. "Private Investment and the Institutionalization of Collective Action in Autocracies: Ruling Parties and Legislatures." *Journal of Politics* 74(2): 621–635. doi: 10.1017/S0022381611001952.

Gigerenzer, Gerd, and Peter M. Todd, with the ABC Research Group. 1999. *Simple Heuristics That Make Us Smart*. Oxford: Oxford University Press.

Golden, Miriam, and Brian Min. 2013. "Distributive Politics Around the World." *Annual Review of Political Science* 16(1): 73–99. doi: 10.1146/annurev-polisci-052209-121553.

Guasch, J. Luis. 2004. "Granting and Renegotiating Infrastructure Concessions: Doing it Right." Washington, DC: World Bank. doi: 10.1596/0-8213-5792-1.

Guzman, Jorge, and Scott Stern. 2015. "Where Is Silicon Valley?" *American Association for the Advancement of Science* 347(6222): 606–609. doi: 10.1126/science.aaa0201.

Haggard, Stephan, Andrew MacIntyre, and Lydia Tiede. 2008. "The Rule of Law and Economic Development." *Annual Review of Political Science* 11 (2008): 205–234.

Hanneman, Robert, and Mark Riddle. 2005. *Introduction to Social Network Methods*. Riverside, CA: University of California, Riverside. http://faculty.ucr.edu/~hanneman/nettext/.

Henisz, Witold J. 2000. "The Institutional Environment for Economic Growth." *Economics and Politics* 12(1): 1–31. doi: 10.1111/1468-0343.00066.

Herics, Oskar, Thomas Obermayr, Pietro Puricella, et al. 2018. "Special Report: Private Partnerships in the EU: Widespread Shortcomings and Limited Benefits." *European Court of Auditors*. https://op.europa.eu/webpub/eca/special-reports/ppp-9-2018/en/.

Hodge, Graeme A., and Carsten Greve. 2007. "Public–Private Partnerships: An International Performance Review." *Public Administration Review* 67(3): 545–558. doi: 10.1111/j.1540-6210.2007.00736.x.

2011. "A Transformative Perspective on Public–Private Partnerships." In *The Ashgate Research Companion to the New Public Management*. London: Ashgate Publishing Ltd., 265–277.

Hood, Christopher. 1991. "A Public Management for All Seasons?" *Public Administration* 69(1): 3–19.

House of Commons Library. 1997. The National Health Service (Private Finance) Bill [HL] Bill 38 of 1997/98, Research Paper 97/88, July 9, 1997: https://commonslibrary.parliament.uk/research-briefings/rp97-88/.

Huber, John D., and Charles R. Shipan. 2002. *Deliberate Discretion: The Institutional Foundations of Bureaucratic Autonomy.* New York: Cambridge University Press.

Hvidman, Ulrik, and Simon Calmar Andersen. 2015. "Perceptions of Public and Private Performance: Evidence from a Survey Experiment." *Public Administration Review* 76(1): 111–120. doi: 10.1111/puar.12441.

Iossa, Elisabetta, and David Martimort. 2012. "Risk Allocation and the Costs and Benefits of Public–Private Partnerships." *The Rand Journal of Economics* 43(3): 442–474. doi: 10.1111/j.1756-2171.2012.00181.x.

2015. "The Simple Microeconomics of Public–Private Partnerships." *Journal of Public Economic Theory* 17(1): 4–48. doi: 10.1111/jpet.12114.

2016. "Corruption in PPPs, Incentives and Contract Incompleteness." *International Journal of Industrial Organization* 44: 85–100. doi: 10.1016/j.ijindorg.2015.10.007.

Kahneman, Daniel. 2011. *Thinking, Fast and Slow.* New York: Farrar, Straus and Giroux.

Kam, Christopher, Anthony Michael Bertelli, and Alexander Held. 2020. "The Electoral System, the Party System, and Accountability in Parliamentary Government." *American Political Science Review* 114(3): 744–760. doi: 10.1017/S0003055420000143.

Kaufmann, Daniel, Aart Kraay, and Massimo Mastruzzi. 2010. "The Worldwide Governance Indicators: Methodology and Analytical Issues." World Bank Policy Research Working Paper No. 5430. https://ssrn.com/abstract=1682130.

Klijn, Erik Hans, and Geert R. Teisman. 2003. "Institutional and Strategic Barriers to Public–Private Partnership: An Analysis of Dutch Cases." *Public Money and Management* 23(3): 137–146. doi: 10.1111/1467-9302.00361.

Leff, Nathan. 1964. "Economic Development through Bureaucratic Corruption." *American Behavioral Scientist* 8(3), 8–14.

Lobina, Emanuele. 2005. "Problems with Private Water Concessions: A Review of Experiences and Analysis of Dynamics." *International Journal of Water Resources Development* 21(1): 55–87. doi: 10.1080/0790062042000313304.

Lynn Jr., Laurence E. 1998. "The New Public Management: How to Transform a Theme into a Legacy." *Public Administration Review* 58(3): 231–237.

Manin, Bernard. 1997. *The Principles of Representative Government.* New York: Cambridge University Press.

Martimort, David, and Jerome Pouyet. 2008. "To Build or Not to Build: Normative and Positive Theories of Public–Private Partnerships." *International Journal of Industrial Organization* 26(2): 393–411. doi: 10.1016/j.ijindorg.2006.10.004.

Marvel, John D. 2015a. "Public Opinion and Public Sector Performance: Are Individuals' Beliefs about Performance Evidence-Based or the Product of Anti-public Sector Bias?" *International Public Management Journal* 18(2): 209–227. doi: 10.1080/10967494.2014.996627.

2015b. "Unconscious Bias in Citizens' Evaluations of Public Sector Performance." *Journal of Public Administration Research and Theory* 26 (1): 143–158. doi: 10.1093/jopart/muu053.

Milgrom, Paul R., Douglass C. North, and Barry R. Weingast. 1990. "The Role of Institutions in the Revival of Trade: The Medieval Law Merchant." *Economics and Politics* 2(1): 1–23. doi: 10.1111/j.1468-0343.1990.tb00020.x.

Milward, H. Brinton, and Keith G. Provan. 1998. "Principles for Controlling Agents: The Political Economy of Network Structure." *Journal of Public Administration Research and Theory* 8(2): 203–222. doi: 10.1093/oxford-journals.jpart.a024378.

Moore, Mark A., Anthony E. Boardman, and Aidan R. Vining. 2017. "Analyzing Risk in PPP Provision of Utility Services: A Social Welfare Perspective." *Utilities Policy* 48(October): 210–218. doi: 10.1016/j.jup.2017.08.008.

Nelson, Richard R., and Winter, Sidney G. 1982. *An Evolutionary Theory of Economic Change.* Cambridge, MA: Belknap Press of Harvard University Press.

Newman, Mark. 2006. "Finding Community Structure in Networks Using the Eigenvectors of Matrices." *Physical Review* 74(3): 1–19. doi: 10.1103/PhysRevE.74.036104.

2018. *Networks.* Oxford: Oxford University Press.

New York Times. 2020. "Was the Pfizer Vaccine Part of the Government's Operation Warp Speed?" November 10. www.nytimes.com/2020/11/10/health/was-the-pfizer-vaccine-part-of-the-governments-operation-warp-speed.html.

Ng, A., and Martin Loosemore. 2007. "Risk Allocation in the Private Provision of Public Infrastructure." *International Journal of Project Management* 25 (1): 66–76. doi: 10.1016/j.ijproman.2006.06.005.

North, Douglass C. 1990. *Institutions, Institutional Change and Economic Performance*. New York: Cambridge University Press. doi: 10.1017/ CBO9780511808678.

OECD. 2018. *Multi-level Governance Studies Subnational Public–Private Partnership: Meeting Infrastructure Challenges*. Paris: OECD Publishing.

Ohashi, Hiroshi. 2009. "Effects of Transparency in Procurement Practices on Government Expenditure: A Case Study of Municipal Public Works." *Review of Industrial Organization* 34(3): 267–285. doi: 10.1007/s11151-009-9208-1.

Pfizer Inc. 2020. "Pfizer and BioNTech Announce Vaccine Candidate against COVID-19 Achieved Success in First Interim Analysis from Phase 3 Study." November 9. www.pfizer.com/news/press-release/press-release-detail/pfizer-and-biontech-announce-vaccine-candidate-against.

Polanyi, Michael. 1966. *The Tacit Dimension*. Chicago: University of Chicago Press.

Porter, Michael E. 1990. "The Competitive Advantage of Nations." *Competitive Intelligence Review* 1:1 14.

1998. "Clusters and the New Economics of Competition." *Harvard Business Review* 76(6): 77–90.

Post, Alison E. 2014. *Foreign and Domestic Investment in Argentina: The Politics of Privatized Infrastructure*. Cambridge: Cambridge University Press. doi: 10.1017/CBO9781107256569.

Provan, Keith G., and H. Brinton Milward. 1995. "A Preliminary Theory of Interorganizational Network Effectiveness: A Comparative Study of Four Community Mental Health Systems." *Administrative Science Quarterly* 40(1): 1–33. doi: 10.2307/2393698.

2001. "Do Networks Really Work? A Framework for Evaluating Public-Sector Organizational Networks." *Public Administration Review* 61(4): 414–423. doi: 10.1111/0033-3352.00045.

Quelin, Bertrand V., Sandro Cabral, Sergio Lazzarini, and Ilze Kivleniece. 2019. "The Private Scope in Public–Private Collaborations: An Institutional and Capability-Based Perspective." *Organization Science* 30(4): 831–846. doi: 10.1287/orsc.2018.1251.

Savas, E. S. 2000. *Privatization and Public–Private Partnerships*. New York: Chatham House.

Sheffey, Ayelet. 2021. "Kristi Noem's Statement on Pipes Not Being Infrastructure Sums Up Her Party's Confused Reaction to Biden's Plan." *Business Insider*, April 2. www.businessinsider.com/kristi-noem-infrastructure-pipes-south-dakota-governor-republicans-fox-news-2021-4.

Simon, Herbert A. 1956. "Rational Choice and the Structure of the Environment." *Psychological Review* 63(2): 129–138. doi: 10.1037/h0042769.

Sparrow, Andrew. 2011. "George Osborne Backs 61 PFI Projects Despite Earlier Doubts Over Costing." *The Guardian*, April 17. www.theguardian.com/politics/2011/apr/18/george-osborne-backs-pfi-projects.

Tankersley, Jim, and Jeanna Smialek. 2021. "Biden Plan Spurs Fight Over What 'Infrastructure' Really Means." *New York Times*, April 5. www.nytimes.com/2021/04/05/business/economy/biden-infrastructure.html.

Teorell, Jan, Stefan Dahlberg, Sören Holmberg, et al. 2020. "The Quality of Government Standard Dataset, Version Jan20." *University of Gothenburg: The Quality of Government Institute.* doi: 10.18157/qogstdjan20.

Thomas Bohlken, Anjali. 2019. "Development or Rent Seeking? How Political Influence Shapes Public Works Provision in India." *British Journal of Political Science* 51(1): 253–274. doi: 10.1017/s0007123418000376.

Turrini, Alex, Daniela Cristofoli, Francesca Frosini, and Greta Nasi. 2010. "Networking Literature about Determinants of Network Effectiveness." *Public Administration* 88(2): 528–550. doi: 10.1111/j.1467-9299.2009.01791.x.

US Department of Health and Human Services. 2021. "Fact Sheet: Explaining Operation Warp Speed." January 21. www.hhs.gov/coronavirus/explaining-operation-warp-speed/index.html.

Vining, Aidan R., and Anthony E. Boardman. 2008. "Public–Private Partnerships: Eight Rules for Governments." *Public Works Management & Policy* 13(2): 149–161. doi: 10.1177/1087724X08323843.

Weingast, Barry R., and Mark J. Moran. 1983. "Bureaucratic Discretion or Congressional Control? Regulatory Policymaking by the Federal Trade Commission." *Journal of Political Economy* 91(5): 765–800. doi: 10.1086/261181.

Weingast, Barry R., Kenneth A. Shepsle, and Christopher Johnsen. 1981. "The Political Economy of Benefits and Costs: A Neoclassical Approach to Distributive Politics." *Journal of Political Economy* 89(4): 642–664. doi: 10.1086/260997.

White House. 2020. "Remarks by President Trump during an Update on Operation Warp Speed." www.whitehouse.gov/briefings-statements/remarks-president-trump-update-operation-warp-speed/.

Woodhouse, Eleanor, Paolo Belardinelli, and Anthony M. Bertelli. 2021. "Do Politicians Benefit from Hybrid Governance? Experimental Evidence from the United States" *Journal of Public Administration Research and Theory.* doi: 10.1093/jopart/muab014.

Woodhouse, Eleanor Florence. 2019. "The Distributive Politics of Privately Financed Infrastructure Agreements." Paper presented at the *Annual Meeting of the Midwest Political Science Association*, Chicago, Illinois, April 2019.

Wooldridge, Jeffrey M., 1999. "Distribution-Free Estimation of Some Nonlinear Panel Data Models." *Journal of Econometrics* 90(1): 77–97.

World Bank. 2017. "Public–Private Partnerships: Reference Guide Version 3." Washington, DC: World Bank. https://openknowledge.worldbank.org/han dle/10986/29052.

2019. *H1 2019: Private Participation in Infrastructure (PPI).* https://ppi .worldbank.org/content/dam/PPI/documents/H12019_PPI-report_small.pdf.

Yehoue, Etienne B., Mona Hammami, and Jean-François Ruhashyankiko. 2006. *Determinants of Public–Private Partnerships in Infrastructure.* Washington, DC: International Monetary Fund.

Zhang, Xueqing. 2005. "Critical Success Factors for Public–Private Partnerships in Infrastructure Development." *Journal of Construction Engineering and Management* 131(1): 3–14. doi: 10.1061/(ASCE)0733-9364(2005)131:1(3).

Acknowledgments

We thank Alisha Holland, Paolo Pin, and Julio Ramos Pastrana for very helpful comments on a prior version of this manuscript. Sean Gailmard, Dan Honig, and David Lazer also provided helpful suggestions for which we are grateful. Fiona Cece and Caroline Riegel provided excellent research assistance.

Cambridge Elements ☰

Public and Nonprofit Administration

Andrew Whitford

University of Georgia

Andrew Whitford is Alexander M. Crenshaw Professor of Public Policy in the School of Public and International Affairs at the University of Georgia. His research centers on strategy and innovation in public policy and organization studies.

Robert Christensen

Brigham Young University

Robert Christensen is professor and George Romney Research Fellow in the Marriott School at Brigham Young University. His research focuses on prosocial and antisocial behaviors and attitudes in public and nonprofit organizations.

About the Series

The foundation of this series are cutting-edge contributions on emerging topics and definitive reviews of keystone topics in public and nonprofit administration, especially those that lack longer treatment in textbook or other formats. Among keystone topics of interest for scholars and practitioners of public and nonprofit administration, it covers public management, public budgeting and finance, nonprofit studies, and the interstitial space between the public and nonprofit sectors, along with theoretical and methodological contributions, including quantitative, qualitative and mixed-methods pieces.

The Public Management Research Association

The Public Management Research Association improves public governance by advancing research on public organizations, strengthening links among interdisciplinary scholars, and furthering professional and academic opportunities in public management.

Cambridge Elements ≡

Public and Nonprofit Administration

Elements in the Series

A full series listing is available at: www.cambridge.org/EPNP

Printed in the United States
by Baker & Taylor Publisher Services